Contents

Introduction

If you're looking for another crude college book that is intended just to make you laugh, you should probably look somewhere else. If you're looking for a book that will make the college choice for you, go somewhere else. If you're looking for a book that makes a complicated and hilarious time in your life easier to understand then this is your book. Guess what? You're going to laugh along the way, and I hope that you do.

Universities are a business looking to make money through donations and tuition. But that doesn't mean you can't maximize your bang for the buck while you're there. That is what this book is about.

In my time I have seen the curtains, behind the curtains, and the curtain-making process. I have been an undergraduate student at a small college and a major university. I spent my graduate school days as a classroom instructor at a mid-size (15,000 students) university. Lastly, I have worked for a university and seen how much of a business it really is. As a student I was periodically on the dean's list (finished with a 3.4 combined GPA) at all three institutions I attended, while rarely sacrificing a chance to hang out with friends. I have gathered the advice of many of my other similar friends (dean's list students that seemed to know everyone) and their observations throughout their time in college into this book. It is definitely a challenge to balance your social and academic life while molding yourself into something companies value. Hopefully this book will help you get ahead of the ball and gives you some laughs along the way.

Picking Your University or College

You will see commercials for schools, some you'll follow through their athletics, and some you may have even toured. The commercials focus on the most picturesque part of campus with students of different races throwing a football out in the quad or happily studying together in a comfortable part of the library. There will be some clip about groundbreaking research and having tons of degree options for students to choose from. There may even be a short clip about the athletic teams on campus, a girl thoughtfully examining a test tube, and a clip of the three weeks of acceptable weather that the college town has per year.

But let's knock out one possibility out of the equation from the beginning. You're going to see ads for online colleges that very few employers take seriously. They try to tell you that you'll save time and money by going to their online school, and although that is true, it is hard to take those degrees seriously. Nothing will look as unimpressive as your inability to break out of your shell to go to a big boy college where you actually need to interact with other people. You will also be handicapping yourself socially by avoiding the many interesting people that turn into lifelong friends, and getting involved in organizations.

What you need to know is this kind of like panning for gold; once you finish up and have a few glimmers of gold left 99% of the rest is crap. Colleges are like that and all they want to show you is the gold, not the crappy temporary trailers they have set up on campus for you to have class in or the constant construction you have to walk around for buildings you won't get the chance to enjoy. These trailers will have paper thin walls and no air conditioning in August; it'll be like sitting in an Easy Bake Oven. The truly great schools don't really need commercials, because they can get by on reputation alone. Honestly, how often do you see Harvard or Yale commercials?

You will be able to enjoy many of the things that they use to try to make your campus beautiful; but you won't give a damn about a good 50% of what's available at larger universities. You will be so busy with an academic and social life that you couldn't care less that the school has a great meteorology department. Yes, the school has terrific departments and specialties but so does most every major institution in the country. The rest of the departments are a crap shoot and these are probably one of the programs you will end up in because they aren't mentally draining. But if you're talented, employers will find you. Small schools give you more hands-on experience opportunities and large schools have a widespread group of contacts and a strong sense of competitiveness.

I recommend not jumping into something immediately unless you are 100% sure that is what you want to do. Picking your college should be based off matching your personality more so than a career goal, because college opens your eyes to a lot of different career options you've never considered. Also priorities change from year to year as different doors open, and the job market changes. I never would have guessed I would get a journalism degree when I started college.

You will likely have no idea what you want to really do while you're in high school. If you have the slightest clue, you're ahead of most. You probably have not even been exposed to a great deal of diversity or different educational routes before stepping foot on a campus. In high school, they traditionally give you very little choice of classes you can take to stay on course to graduation. If you were lucky enough to attend a school with a wide variety of choices such as technical schools or discipline focused schools you are probably in better shape. Most high schools offer advanced placement courses or have an agreement with local schools for you to earn college credit. If you can, take advantage of these opportunities. In college the general education classes open up your eyes to a lot of possibilities. You can get your feet wet and go into a major you're passionate about. I love to shape products and this is the reason why I went into journalism, and have worked with start-up companies a lot since.

When picking a college or university, you should look more at your personality than anything. If you're adventurous, take a look all over the country and do your research at websites and request tons of information. If you love Christianity, then a small Christian college is probably for you because there will be very little partying and it will be quiet. If you love your high school friends, you should go somewhere locally. But one thing that I warn about is going to the trendy school along with high school friends, because this will not allow you to explore other people much and it is like signing an extension of your high school career. A quarter of my high school graduating class went to the same college.

Regardless of where you will go you have to understand that what you have accomplished in the past will mean nothing after you have been accepted and step foot on campus. No one you meet will truthfully care if you played high school baseball or you were in National Honor Society. Don't brag about being in the top 20% of your high school class, because most of the people around you will probably have similar accomplishments. Refrain from wearing your varsity jacket, because that is living in the past and grounds for laughter. Once you get into college you're back at the ground floor and have not accomplished anything other than getting in.

Picking your college is huge because it is one of the few chances for you to move wherever you want. If you have dreamed about beaches, this is your chance to look at schools like Miami, San Diego State, Hawaii, etc.; or you love college football, research Penn State, Ohio State, Alabama, Florida, etc. Just try to figure out what it is that you really love to do in your spare time and find a school that has these qualities. You have a lot of downtime in college to fill in activities and clubs to not only satisfy your passions but also build a resume. Time management and responsibility will easily be the greatest skills you learn.

Once you are able to put together a list of loves, start researching your butt off to find schools that best fits your mold. Some people like the small town feel of a college where they can see and work with the same people every day. Some people like diversity and ethnic experiences they will receive at a larger university, but I can't stress doing as much research as possible. Some high schools will give you a handful of excusable school days you can take off (typically five) to tour campuses, so you should take advantage of these opportunities and really get a feel for what the school is about. Ask lots of questions while you're there.

Colleges will be vying to make you spend thousands of dollars a year on their education, so you better pick the place that best suits you and your situation. Don't let people influence you to go one place or another; in the end it is you who is investing the time and money. You should factor in academics, but because most of my friends changed their major at one time or another, I would not put that responsibility into 17-year-old hands. It really just is far too difficult to know what you want to do for the rest of your life at that age. I wouldn't recommend even declaring a major until 2-3 semesters into college.

If you are lucky, the school will offer you financial incentive. I highly recommend taking this route as most of my friends, years out of school, are still paying loans. The sooner you can get back to breaking even, the better. As I said before you can be successful anywhere, if you network and work hard to build a professional portfolio. Don't let someone put you down because they are going to a fancier school. If you put together a good enough professional portfolio of work related to your industry, you can succeed coming out of anywhere.

To tell you the truth, if you can't find what you want to do at a college or a university with all their random academic programs and disciplines you're probably too picky. If you're good at what it is you do, jobs and graduate schools will be able to find you. Don't be discouraged if it takes a while and keep plugging away getting your name out there. The name will help a little, but not enough to warrant the cost of going to a Harvard over a full scholarship to Ohio State. Cream always rises to the top, and if you work hard enough wherever you go it will pay off. Networking and hard work will make you the cream of the crop whether you go to Columbia or Joe Blow University. In a tie, I'd give the significant edge to Columbia.

The last thing you want to do is end up somewhere where you will be miserable and will transfer. This stinks because not all credits transfer and it could keep you in college an extra semester or two and cost you even more money that you could have saved from the start. I can't emphasize more **Do your research and go somewhere that fits what you want,** because listening to other people will screw you over. Only you know what you're interested in, not your girlfriend, parents, brother and sisters, or friends. They know you, but no one really knows everything someone is thinking.

I've been to three campuses in my five years of college: Penn State-Altoona, Penn State-University Park, and Southern Mississippi.

They are all very different in their own way, so I will try to give the best description I can of each campus so you could possibly relate to a type of campus you enjoy. I think understanding the size of the campus is far more important than the type of school (private vs. public).

My first two years were at Penn State-Altoona from 2004 to 2006, which is a small division three college of about 4,500 people, mainly used as a purgatory of sorts for those waiting to go to University Park. Most people do transfer from PSU-Altoona to University Park after two years, but it is only 40 minutes from University Park so students have a chance to go to sporting events and get acclimated with campus before attending the school. It is a nice stepping-stone, especially for someone coming from a really rural area and is not used to the hustle and bustle of a large city or lots of people.

The classes were fairly easy and the class sizes were small, so you were brought along slowly in your first year or two. The campus is fairly small as you can walk from one corner to the other in about 15 minutes, which isn't killer in case you wake up late for class. You will also get sick of the food; because like most small campuses you only have one cafeteria despite the fact it could be good food. Luckily, because the campus was located within a small city, there were a number of restaurants readily available off campus.

You will see the same people every day, which can be a good and a bad thing, depending on the type of person you are. If you are someone that likes meeting a variety of people, small schools are not the place for you. But if you are someone who possibly might not know many or any people going into college life this could be your place. Being at a small campus really accelerates the friendships. The problem with a small campus is that most kids go home on the weekend. So there will be even less people on the weekend; for me it led to a lot of beers, football, and Texas Hold Em' games.

My next stop took me to Penn State-University Park, which is a campus that dwarfs Penn State-Altoona in every aspect of the word. I felt like a freshman again stepping foot onto campus and moving into my off-campus apartment, which was only a short walk away from campus and nightlife. This campus truly gave you a little bit of everything as the town of State College is tightly wrapped around the campus. You can go weeks without ever needing a car, but there are buses available free on campus and in downtown area where I lived. Buses are necessary because of the size of the campus, which takes about 40-45 minutes to walk from corner to corner.

There is an organization for just about everything at University Park and the intramural competition was more competitive than what I experienced at Altoona, where we were perennial playoff contenders in every sport. The resources are tremendous, as are the facilities even, if some of the older classrooms leave something to be desired. It is not unusual to hear 6-8 different languages on one walk across campus as students and professors talk to friends and on their phones.

Downtown is just a short walk down the hill from the most picturesque parts of the campus where you can find just about any food to match your hunger. Everything from Indian, Korean, Japanese, Chinese, Austrian, Philadelphia cheese steaks, New York pizza, and much more will often leave you wondering on what you want to get next. I was there a little over two years and did not have the time to eat at every place downtown; although I would like to continue my pursuit to eat at a lot of the places when I go back to visit.

Penn State-Altoona has a pretty solid social life in its apartment complexes, but nothing like Penn State's downtown region, which has a cluster of bars and apartment complexes lining Beaver and College Avenues. Everywhere you look you will see people carrying a slice of pizza or a burger on their way to or from a night out. There is an assortment of types of bars and clubs that can suit just about anyone's taste. If you meet even a handful of people, you will be challenged to go to every party in a given night. Often times my friends and I had 4-6 places to go in any given night. That is what makes Penn State-University Park one of the country's biggest party schools. But college is only a little bit about letting off steam. It is more about shaping who you are.

The academics make you work hard, which is part of the reason why a lot of people party harder than other places. The academics and competition for internships is extremely tough, which demands a great deal of hard work to distinguish you in a campus of this size. The level of the bar set in many of the programs will make you elevate your work ethic out of necessity, and outside programs will be impressed when you go against candidates from other universities. Everything at a big school is competitive and it'll make you a better person.

Lastly, I went to the University of Southern Mississippi for a year to collect my master's degree in sport management. This is a campus that fits in between Penn State-Altoona and Penn State-University Park in relation to size. During the week it resembled University Park, and the very busy campus setting where you rarely see the same person twice in the same day, but during the weekend it was much like Penn State-Altoona because everyone went home. After being spoiled with the strong social life at PSU, I was disappointed with my early weekends at Southern Miss.

Despite the disappointing social life that exists at Southern Miss, there is beautiful weather and even more beautiful girls. I think my neck was sore within my first three hours on campus and did not get rest until the weekend when all the girls went home. Despite their lack of nightlife, the southern hospitality was tremendous. The food that was down there did not make me miss cheese steaks and good pizza as badly as I thought it would. I fell in love with gumbo, real fried chicken, hot sauces, and I now despise seafood from any place but there.

The campus is fairly compact where you can walk corner to corner in about 20-25 minutes depending on how hot it is. Sometimes I swear the devil wakes up in hell, goes out to his balcony and says, "Wow, it's hotter than Mississippi out here." The intramural sports were a great deal of fun where every team at least had a legitimate chance of winning, unlike Penn State where some teams were stacked good enough to compete with other college varsity squads. The bars, however, were spread out throughout the town, which was tough because you needed a designated driver. It was definitely not a college town atmosphere. The university was a working part of a bigger city.

The campus is surrounded by major highways, thus its name is the Hub City. The town isn't very pedestrian friendly and it is darn near impossible to walk anywhere. That does not mean that everyone is lazy like national statistics seem to say -- Mississippi is often listed as one of the fattest states. It is kind of a twisted statistic because people are either really big or they're really fit, there is very little middle ground. But the culture down there for me was something I haven't really experienced; I can't compare it as better as or worse than Pennsylvania because that is a tough thing to do. It was just different.

I have provided information from a small college, a large university, and a mid-size university for you as honestly as possible. It is up to you to figure out what you are about and what you want out of your college experience. You may not want the shock factor of a public non-religious affiliated college and all the types of people that come with it that you are looking for. But on the other hand, you may want to experience all types of cultures and people; you and only you know what you want. But 50 years down the road, the education is not what you will remember when you pick where you want to be.

Picking the type of campus you want to go to is very important, but regardless of where you'll go, you will form tight relationships with people you meet. It is simply about spending as little time in your room as possible, and getting out and socializing that make the college experience worth the money and effort. There are a lot of people who stay in their room all the time and just think college is another job. These people can't be more wrong.

College is about scraping together enough money for a case of beer or a pizza with your pals and enjoying the night. Spending the night on someone's floor or on a crappy couch is pretty standard in college. You better believe there will be nine people crammed in a two-person room just for the opportunity to party together and have some laughs. You will certainly fight to sleep on that couch and sleep under a jacket or two in your day. It's also about skipping a class or two to take a road trip or throw a football around on a nice day.

Picking Your Major and the Stereotypes That Go Along With Those Majors

WARNING: *If you're a freshman, stop twirling your lanyard around your finger and put it back in your pocket. When you do this you mine as well be wearing a shirt that says "Freshman" on it. Knock it off.*

Everyone always makes a big deal about what you're major is or will be when you pack up mom and dad's car to go to college. None of that matters until the start of the 4th semester, that's roughly 16 months of thinking about what you want to do. The questions about being asked about your major are insanity, because of the relatively small amount of life experience you've accumulated. I wanted to be a professional baseball player, and I was 5'9" 130 pounds if that sheds any light on the pressure put on high school kids to choose a career. I had zero idea what I wanted to be.

I just had a limited selection of classes in high school that gave me an outlook on life. I didn't really know what it took to get certain jobs, how to make a resume or a cover letter to apply for those jobs. High school really just made me decide what general areas I completely hate and will avoid in college. I was an absolutely awful science and foreign language student; so I took the easiest routes in those fields to fulfill my general education requirements and then got out of dodge.

I hated reading going into college, an activity I have changed my mind about since now that I have discovered a variety of quality authors. Now I read 35 books a year. I knew that history classes were a ton of reading, so I stayed away from history classes in college and actually never took one in five years. I was able to find alternate classes in the registrar to supplement the classes that gave me the opportunity to watch a bunch of movies instead. I took Russian, German, and French culture classes in my first two years from people who had spent a great deal of time in the country which was extremely interesting. The information I learned in these classes has actually come in handy in conversations later on down the road.

I knew going into college that I didn't hate English, gym class, and business, and I loved sports. So I started out with a really general degree choice in Communications, only because I did not feel like taking economics because I hated that class in high school. Now that I have taken a number of classes in business either route I took as an 18-year-old I do not regret. Eventually, I settled into sports journalism during my sophomore year, which meant I got to cover a lot of the very highly exposed Penn State athletics at University Park.

People choose majors usually for one of three reasons. The first of these is they really know what they want to do because they have a passion for something, which is really what you should follow. There is another group of people who pick a major because they know there is lots of money and prestige in the position, and pursue it because they want the good life. Lastly, there are people who pick a major because they hear the classes to getting the degree are easy.

Most people change their major a time or two; and now looking back in retrospect of the current economy it might have been good if I did. I ended up with a degree in journalism, and in my last semester I found out it was the lowest paying profession of any major at Penn State. I wanted to go out and get a pitcher of beer after that comment; too bad the bar was closed at 9:15 AM.

I took the route somewhere between doing what I wanted and what was easy. I really had no connections in the field, or any field for that matter. There really is not much industry where I am from and I was far from a country club type growing up. It took me time to develop networking skills that turn out to be the most important skill you develop in college, even more than your grades. It is who you know 75% of the time and what you know 25% of the time.

Try to pick a major in a field where you know some people for an early internship or two to develop your resume. Your resume should be like your Facebook page; being updated constantly to paint the best portrait of you for those who will view it. Getting the first job in the field is always the toughest one to obtain; so making early contacts are decisive for your future. Sucking up is not recommended, but you got to do what you got to do. Saving your pride is not worth working at Arby's at age 25 with a bachelor's degree.

While at Penn State I also acquired a movement sciences minor degree, which just a fancy way of saying I learned about coaching and Greek culture. I still wanted a bit of the business end of sports so I went to Southern Mississippi on a graduate assistant position to get a master's degree in sports management. I have been able to chisel the skills that I enjoyed coming out of high school. Much like choosing the university or college of your choice it is important to figure out what you like to do, or in my case don't hate doing.

Throughout your high school career and early college days you will find out what it is that you hate to do by doing stupid and sometimes demeaning jobs. There simply are subjects some people never grasp on, like it is easy for me to explain how athletics and economics work in sports, but to someone else I might as well be speaking Chinese. But it is the same for me listening to someone talk about complex political issues that I can only add to marginally at best.

Engineering

I hope you like spending endless hours in a studio somewhere while you're hopped on Mountain Dew and very rarely can go out. This major demands an extreme amount of patience, good art skills, and a well-developed understanding of math. You will also be constantly surrounded by guys, most of whom have no idea how to talk to a woman. Engineers are constantly on the verge of losing their minds and hair. The only thing that keeps them sane is the fact they will probably be making more money than just about everyone else.

You will need a hard hat, large backpack, and pockets large enough for a graphing calculator and most likely a protractor, and also need to wear jeans all the time. Your body will learn to run off of caffeine as you slowly lose your hair from a combination of malnutrition and stress. You will probably also gain bad weight with all the time spent at the vending machines, but you know it will all be worth it in the end when you work for a firm and can get a woman who doesn't care about looks. Some may call her a trophy wife.

These are the people who were able to step their game up enough to laugh at the ITT Tech graduates in the face. Although a nerdy group, they do come in handy when you can wrangle them out to a bar because they know all engineering feats because they own the DVD series Modern Marvels. While you couldn't give a damn about the difference between Roman and Gothic architecture these people can not only tell the difference, but give you a five minute synopsis. They're also good guys to know when you eventually need to buy a home or office. My roommate was an engineering major.

Communications

Now this is the department where I got my undergraduate degree, so this is the discipline where I'll have the most expertise to give. People in Communications typically do not like waking up early in the morning, and in our case we didn't even have class on Friday's. But you tend to get a wide variety of people in Communications, with more than half being girls. You have people working in television, radio, print, public relations, advertising, telecommunications, film, or a general communications discipline. There tends to be a good amount of great looking girls, particularly ones who want to be in television. They will get jobs over you because even if you have comparable resumes, employers will pick what will draw in viewers.

Despite these many great looking girls being in your field, not many will talk to you because they are holding out for something and someone better. We know that we will struggle financially out of college, but will have a blast producing our own content. There are a fair number of artistic people particularly in film and broadcasting with their canvas being electronic files they spend hours perfecting. As a broadcast journalist, I spent a lot of time in the lab perfecting my craft and making sound bytes for my radio show.

The oddest of all the groups is probably the film people, because they are all looking to be the next Stanley Kubrick with new inventive camera angles and techniques. Their uniqueness is often their greatest social flaw as others will view them with a look of skepticism as they talk about some obscure filmmaker of from Sundance Film Festival that no one has heard of. Yes, we realize that our university is just a stopping ground or a roadblock between you and your successful career in film in Hollywood. But their uniqueness is their tool to success.

As a writer, almost everyone in the field drinks because of the extreme deadlines you are forced to deal with and the need to talk out ideas. While your other roommates have two weeks to put together a power point presentation, a writer has to go to a town meeting at 9 PM that doesn't end until 10:15. Then you have to return and write a feature of 600 words that is due by midnight, which is usually chased by a shot of Jim Beam as the adrenaline wears off. You don't work all day, but when you do it is under extreme conditions that sometimes are out of your control.

With the public relations and advertising people they typically are the people (85% girls) who are the small town girls looking to make a big city impression. Hollywood (aka. The Film majors) has made countless films about these girls having to stress and fight for internships in New York City making contacts and meeting the man of their dreams. If you want to be in a small town, do not even consider this as a major unless you want to write up the classifieds for some backwoods' paper.

Business

A good number of these people have seen the movie "Boiler Room" one too many times and naturally think business is a cut-throat industry. In some respects they are correct, but not everyone is made out of the CEO mold coming out of college. Yet, these business folks think that they all have some grand idea that will be influential to the industry that they choose.

Business majors are easy to spot. They will rattle off the top 20 companies to work for in the country despite the fact that you don't give a damn. They are the ones in large groups at restaurant chains they feel are classy and they admire their complex vision statement; most likely Chili's, Ruby Tuesday's, TGI Friday's, and Applebee's. They will be fed up with their careers when they are forced into a sales position that requires them to cold call people and explain their product. I have worked in sales, and it definitely takes a special type of personality and ability to want to refrain from screaming to yourself in your car during a break.

You will know these kids also because they feel it is necessary to carry around copies of Consumer Reports, Wall Street Journal, and Fortune magazine to impress others with their business savvy. They can tell you about macroeconomics and ambush marketing until they're purple in the face. You're almost guaranteed to find at least one Wall Street ticker somewhere in their honey nest educational setting as they talk about the strength of the dollar. Naturally, you will pretend to pay attention and nod.

However, they will probably have the most jobs to pick from when they graduate. The problem is that there are so many of them that the jobs all get 200 resumes so making yourself stand out becomes even more important. These people usually see all the angles and will tell you about it whether you care or not.

Liberal Arts

These people will most likely be weird, I mean really weird. They will name off old time movies and Broadway shows that you have never heard of and do not care to see. They will also often critique acting in movies because they've been through four semesters of theater taught by some local former actor. Parts of the theater to you will become ingrained in your head as you're trying to ignore their worthless ramblings about tone and accents.

However, despite being weird, the girls will be attractive, and I mean really good looking because they want to look good for their head shots and auditions. Be prepared for emotions from a character to carry over into their everyday life though, which will often leave you scratching your head. But they claim it helps with their development of the character because they heard Betty White mention it on the Actors' Guild presentation on some random film site online. These girls will probably be into dieting and will look good for a long time, so putting up with weird personality issues is worth the effort.

There will be a lot of gay guys in this field, who will always hang out with the girls in their major. Most of these guys will probably be pretty cool; but every now and then you will run into the Mr. Fabulous who will tear up your sense of style and lack of pop culture knowledge. It will be like a live version of Queer Eye for the Straight Guy. Despite his many insults you would still feel bad punching him squarely in the face.

These people will obviously be very artistic and if you stay close to them could be useful when decorating your house and hooking you up with tickets. They are extremely talented, but they are usually odd and set in their ways. These artistic people will blow your mind with creativity, despite the insane cost of their products that may only attract rich European aristocrats and venture capitalists.

Education

These people are usually cautious in their early college days drinking because of the knowledge being given a citation for underage could mean getting booted from the program. They will be insanely cautious at every party, and bail at any signs of cops showing up. I once saw an education major jump off a second story balcony when security guards (not the cops) showed up.

But as soon as they turn 21, watch out because they probably will be tanked out of their gourds on any night that does not get followed by a day of student teaching. They will be the ones doing a lifetime worth of drinking in two years while you spread it out; it won't be unusual to get a call from education majors to go out to the bar on a Tuesday night. You will be asking what is wrong with this person and will join them anyways.

Most of the people who are in the major would make good parents and can handle kids, which is something I admire because I'm exhausted after having to watch a 7 year-old for any longer than 20 minutes. Putting up with 125 of these kids gives you the understanding of why they give teachers three months off every summer, because you would be drinking your life away every night with the knowledge of the next day of school.

The education majors really do not need to have an education any higher than the grade they will teach, which is ideal for elementary education majors. This is a joke of course. You need at least a bachelor's degree to teach. Some high schools even push for a master's degree. Sitting around playing with markers and eating the occasional tube of paste sounds like an exciting venture. They will often bring back projects they made in class including hand print turkeys, cotton ball snowmen, and pilgrim hats, which will be magnetically placed on your fridge.

Criminal Justice

These are the people who probably don't really know what they want to do, but they certainly love the NCIS and CSI shows on television. They may have a police officer in the family but wanted to take it the extra step over the academy by getting a college degree in police work. They can't wait to carry a gun, badge, suspenders, a shirt and a tie to work so they can crack some big case by pressuring a suspect in an interrogation room.

They either have those high hopes or they come from a family of criminals and simply just want to learn the cutting edge of police work. They will then take this knowledge back to the family to tie up loose ends in their industry that may be exploited and take care of them. This will last until the next child in the family gets old enough to go to college and mend more holes in the family business. I'm kidding, I've never heard of this.

These people are all about public service, which is honorable, but the characters I know going into this field are all over the board. I see ROTC all the way to the guys who you never see going to class and just sit out on the stoop taking in the college life until they fail out. All of them believe in the adult version of the games cops and robbers that awaits them after graduation. The goal is to be on an episode of COPS after all; it doesn't matter if it's as the cop or the robber.

Sciences/Pre-Med

These people will probably be the craziest you meet in college, but only because they are dealing with words that are obscenely long and having to memorize 75 cards with various bacteria on them. The men will make it through the program with an ulcer or two and probably thinning hair, while the girls will have hypertension. Regardless, they will all probably be very high-strung dealing with hurdle after hurdle of complex knowledge.

They will constantly be reminding you how miserable their choice of major was, but how it will be worth it in the end after coughing up eight years of their life. It is true they will probably be making far more money than you will, but you also won't have a tick and have to deal with deadly chemicals on a daily basis, unless you go into the port-a-potty business. Science and pre-med majors will often get praise from parents, family friends, and grandparents who admire what they are doing. The only problem is that they have their nose stuck in a book with 40 page chapters; and the only chemicals they are mixing are Jack and Coke.

A great number of these people will start these majors, but few will finish. Most will retire the thought of being a doctor or physics professor somewhere during their junior year and will switch over to environmental sciences or recreational management to be a park ranger. They've given up the dream in order to keep their hair and salvage some fun out of their early 20's. Not a poor decision if you ask me.

Literature (sometimes linked with Liberal Arts above)

These are the people who hang out in the library because they absolutely adore certain authors who have been dead for 300 years. Despite the talent of the author you probably can't stand the stuff because it is written in medieval language that you don't even want to start to understand. Most people complain about writing a 1,000 word essay for a class about the exciting world anaerobic respiration, but these people will turn it into a haiku or an elaborate 13 page paper because they can find deeper meaning.

No one knows if library science is under this major, and no one majors in that, so it doesn't matter. Don't try to be a pioneer and be the first jerk to ever major in the Dewey Decimal system that make 11 year old children fall asleep at their 6th grade library table (believe me, I was one of those kids). These people will go on to be that creepy old man or librarian that hangs out wearing festive sweaters and tells you the shush with no one else around to disturb.

Those who are really ambitious will go on to write for television and writing books that are better than mine. But, they will probably drink plenty of brandy and whiskey in the pursuit of stardom. Some of them reach stardom, but they will still be a bore to hang out with, because their work will be pulling them away from living a relaxed, normal life. They will constantly be coming up with ideas that they believe are genius.

Law

These characters are like business majors on steroids and high levels of caffeine. They are for the most part interested in having a lavish lifestyle, and willing to cough up their youthful years so they can drink scotch from a crystal glass at the country club when they're 55. The Pre-Law majors will be the only ones in the library more than the library science majors as they cram their heads with worthless knowledge from 35 page court reports from a case in 1947. They will also make their girlfriend think they are cheating on them because they are gone so long making copies and searching obscure books.

The law degree seekers are the ones who love to solve puzzles and crack a case. It's the reason why America loves cinematic masterpieces such as My Cousin Vinnie, A Few Good Men, and of course the lovable Matlock series. It is also the reason why Law and Order has been on television for 400 years and has morphed and bred itself into having anywhere from 31-47 spin-off shows. America would rather watch L.A. Law than watch Des Moines Pool Cleaners, because lawyers make bank and work in a high stress environment. That makes their profession sexy.

Women will be impressed with the guys who fire out the pre-law major out at the bar; however, she will have to put up with the loss of hair and body build in exchange for money and a more comfortable life. Some women are willing to put up with this, while others would rather live with an elementary school gym teacher who doesn't make much but is well built. If you make it out without a tick, high blood pressure, and sleep deprivation while keeping your hair, you're golden.

Philosophy

These characters can never give you a straight answer because there is always a deeper question. But once you address that one, you're branded a communist or a possible serial killer and you don't understand why. These people love sitting around and talking deeply about various subjects and see how they intertwine and while losing 99.9% of the room. There is a high degree of connection between different subjects and historical events that the majority of mankind could not care less about, but these characters will connect the dots and team up with Literature majors to write movies like "National Treasure."

Their mindless dribble will only make sense to those of their own kind or those deeply involved in the subject they are talking about. But the rest of us are asleep somewhere on a couch trying to make it through the foreword of their publications. All of their tests will be essay based and if you are a terrific and a PhD candidate in BS than this maybe your field. If you can ramble on and on about deeper meanings and symbolism, than you will probably score highly on the tests that are given to you. Or simply put the question "Why?" on the test and walk out of the room. You'll probably still get an 88%.

Kinesiology

Grab your basketball shorts and a t-shirt because you will have the most relaxed dress code of any of the majors on campus. You get to hang out in the gym all day and learn how to teach dodge ball, wrap injuries, and learn how athletic movement works. You will deal with lots of sciences, anatomy, and psychology, all while doing it in an athletic atmosphere. The major will be surprisingly hard because of all that science and anatomy that you will need to learn to achieve the degree to be an athletic trainer, personal trainer, coach, or anything along those lines.

You better be an early riser as well because the majority of these classes meet at 8 AM and on in the morning, but your day will be over early. Also as a guy there will be plenty of great looking girls who are in shape working in this field. Most likely they are former high school athletes who like athletics and want to keep working in them as long as possible. The girls even keep in shape because all the gyms and weight rooms are right there where you have class, so it is a great hookup for yourself.

As mentioned, I have a minor degree in movement sciences and my master's degree is in sport management out of a Human Performance and Recreation department, which is just a fancy way of saying kinesiology. The legislators and jerk lawyers who have taken kinesiology and the management of sports to an unprecedented level.. Now you can't be a baseball coach if you know the game; but you need several clearances, CPR training, playing experiences, 2-3 years experience for a $3,000 a season job. It is frustrating, but a great deal of fun to major in kinesiology.

Dealing With Textbooks and the Bastards Who Sell Them

What is it with these greedy bastards coming out with new editions and charging poor college students $135 for each book? You will also be angered when you buy this book, and the professor tells you later that the book is optional or you barely use it. It makes you want to smack them across the face and question why it was even on the book list that you got through the university website. After leaving the bookstore, prepare to feel violated and protect your new $600 investment with your life. People will go into unlocked rooms and steal textbooks and sell them back for cash.

What is to be understood is that textbooks will probably eat up a good portion of your bank account, and you won't receive much back for them when you sell them back. You will pay $130 for a book; and maybe get $65 back for it under ideal circumstances. The problem is professors and companies are constantly coming out with new editions that are not far off the previous edition. There may be some new pictures, charts, and some re-wording; it's kind of like changing the carpeting in the living room and then claiming you built a new house. So if at all possible avoid even doing business with the on-campus bookstore, unless it is a last resort.

Most universities have a bookstore through a larger book company who provide a book list for students about a month before classes start. The problem is that the search box is not always easy to find when it comes to looking at the campus bookstore's website. They do this intentionally because they don't want you to know your list until you get on campus and buy through them. It's not your college's fault most of the time, so don't hate the players, hate the game.

Poke around the website for the bookstore and you'll eventually stumble onto the search engine to find out what books you need. Check back a couple times so the evil empire of books doesn't sneak a book or two in that will cost you more money later. Take the list and immediately go to an online site that sells textbooks such as Half.com or Amazon.com and buy your books. You will probably save a good $100-$150 per semester this way. Often times you can sell the books for more than what the bookstore is offering as well.

Beware of the dreaded compiled book that is really just 300 pieces of paper kept together by a cheap plastic spiral spine. You won't be able to buy these books online very often, they will cost $70, and the bookstore will not buy them back. They truly are the ultimate rip-off because you think you do not need a book for the class until you show up. It is not a good first impression by the professors to the students. When I taught gym classes at Southern Miss, I eliminated the textbooks because I find them ridiculous when you're doing physical activities.

It is stupid to just sit back and wait until the last minute to get your books because it is more expensive, and you'll have to fight crowds at the shelves and at the cash register. Sometimes you get to the shelves and there aren't any more used ones left so you're screwed into buying a new one. You'll just generally be frustrated, while your roommate already had their box of books and paid far less than you did because they decided to read this book and take my advice. Some people like to wait until they're absolutely sure they will need the book; this is a risky but an effective way to get your books. You will get behind in readings, but you don't do anything the first week anyways so it is a calculated risk. I once was instructed 45 minutes that I would be teaching a section before its first class meeting. Needless to say, we did nothing.

When it comes time to sell them back, check those two sites I mentioned to see what the books you have are selling for. After you get that information, go to the bookstore and find out what they are giving you there. You need to take into account that the online sites take a commission out and never give you enough money to send out the books; also the time to go to the post-office to mail them is a factor. If you will get something comparable at the bookstore sell them back to the school and blow that cash on something fun like a toga party or Christmas presents for your family.

College Classes

Before I went to college I took a tour of several places. Taking tours of Edinboro, Westminster, Slippery Rock, Pittsburgh, Carnegie Mellon, PSU-Hazleton, and a few others gave me a good idea of what I wanted in a school. Since I was a baseball player I wanted a chance to play on the collegiate level. But the baseball dreams were short lived following an injury I sustained in my right shoulder while weight lifting the summer before my freshman year. I took a tour of Penn State-Altoona a couple times before deciding it was the place for me. I was already very familiar with Penn State because of my family members going there since I was a small child. This small central Pennsylvania college was a wonderful experience located in the hills of a once bustling urban center which is known for its railroad system.

I was still not overwhelmingly prepared for college on the academic sense, but I have enough common sense to get by and make up the difference as I went. Some tips I would give to you before starting your first day of college is taking your schedule and walking around campus to find your classrooms. I didn't do this and I was barely on time for my first college class because I could not find the building. If you knew Penn State-Altoona's tiny campus this is an embarrassing thing to have happen to anyone at the age of 18. I would go back and hit myself upside the head if I could.

I was also lucky enough to have some professors that were able to slow down material for the class so that everyone at least had the chance to grasp the concept before moving on. That was the nice thing about having smaller class sizes as a freshman because it takes time to get a grasp of college life during your first semester on campus. It is tough to balance everything that is on your plate now that no one is there to stay on top of you to get up in the morning and get to school. The students who are able to learn from mistakes and make the proper adjustments are the ones who will rise to the top.

I have to thank a professor at Penn State-Altoona who was one of those guys you immediately sweat upon entering their classroom because they might make you look like an idiot at any moment. There is no slacking off and you dread going to the class. He was a man of large stature and could make anybody feel like a little kid caught stealing from the cookie jar. He had a large booming voice that was far too powerful for the small temporary trailer classroom that English was held in.

I would always walk into the classroom and had the seat two back from the front. I was surrounded mostly by other freshmen and a few slacking upperclassmen who had long dodged the class. I was a cocky kid, who thought he knew everything the world had to offer, but when I got my first paper and there was D+ in big red ink on my title page I thought differently. It crushed my spirit, but it probably was one of the best things that could have happened to me. It humbled me, and really started making a difference starting me on the road to confidence instead of cockiness.

I made the adjustments he asked for and my grades started getting steadily better from paper to paper. I would stay after class to ask questions and learn how I could get better, because the light that fired under me late my junior year in high school to get my grades up continued into college. I really wanted to succeed in college because you have more control over what you learn, so you should be more responsible for how you do than in high school. Starting college, you get the bottom of the barrel as far as class selection so you take what you can get.

In fact, that first semester I had a very odd schedule that had a cornucopia of classes from English, Environmental Sciences, which made me put together a variety of assignments including haikus and hiking trips to identify leaves, a Professional Wrestling class that investigated the history of the "sport" and the workings behind the scenes, and a few others. Realistically, in early college it really does not matter what you take, just as long as you get a decent GPA taking these random classes. You will certainly get crappy times and will have less control over influencing your schedule. But that will change as you build credits.

If there is a decent chance you are going to fall asleep in class, don't go. Literally every day from my sophomore year on I would sit at the edge of my bed every morning and weigh the pros and cons of going or not going to class for about 5-7 minutes. If the cons of going far outweighed the pros then I would go back to sleep and rest up. I would take into account what we were going to be doing, weather, my health, what I would need to do later in the day, and how I had slept the previous night.

While at Penn State Altoona, I probably averaged 10-12 missed classes per semester; 2-3 at Penn State-University Park, because I was by that time in my core classes; and 1 per semester at Southern Miss because the weather was terrific and they did not allow absences. But I missed because of a bad cheese steak I ate and then the next semester I skipped to watch the 2009 NIT Championship. Both absences landed me in the doghouse.

If you are going to fall asleep or don't feel well then don't go, and at least e-mail the professor with some stretching of the truth. An example is you being hung over from the night before; say something along the lines of I think I had something yesterday that did not agree with my stomach and I had a rotten night of sleeping. It is the truth, but it doesn't allude to the fact that you were hammered drunk on a Wednesday night at a local club. It was the 25 cent drafts you had that disagreed with your stomach, but according to the e-mail it could have been old lunch meat you had for dinner while studying for that very class.

You don't want to be too drastic saying things like my grandmother passed away because in this age of the Internet anyone can be tracked down. But if you claim to have an ear ache or case of food poisoning than no one will question that, because college professors rarely really care if you show up to their class because they'll still get paid. They're paid based off of performance, the evaluations they undergo and the ratings they receive from students and department head at the end of the semester dictate their future and possibility of tenure

As you get older, you will pick up tools and gain knowledge about the way the university works. You may even be doing some research and stumble upon some loopholes in the system that relieve you of having to do extra work to get your degree. But I will save you the time and tell you my approach I developed over about three semesters during my freshman and sophomore years. I warn the approach works best for general education classes, electives, and early major classes when you have more of a choice on who you have teaching and when the classes are held. By my sophomore year I was scheduling 8-10 people's classes per semester.

Tips for Scheduling Classes

After that first semester I used various sites such as ratemyprofessor.com to find out how other students felt about certain instructors. I became a guru of sorts scheduling class with the registrar (the inventory of classes and availability), while having the rating system of professors, my degree audit (telling me what I still needed to take), and the course-scheduling program up on my screen. I'm fairly certain that launching nuclear missiles was probably an easier process than was scheduling my classes. I had an intricate system like Phil Jackson's triangle offense for his championship Bulls and Lakers teams, but much like Coach Jackson's insight my work led to an easy schedule. I chose teachers who were real sweethearts and tended to be easier graders, thus boosting my GPA.

Picking your classes is really a science more than anything, because you want the class to be a combination of interesting, easy, and not before 11 AM. You won't have much choice early in your college career and will have to swallow the bullet and take an 8 AM class, something all college students fear. Regardless of the fact that you may have started high school at 7:45 AM, 8 AM is still a crushing blow when it isn't guaranteed. The key to the 8 AM class is showing up and doing just enough to get by. Everyone who walks in is going to look like they just sustained the roughest night of their life. Sometimes this includes the instructor.

When scheduling classes you will get screwed less and less the older you get. People have different goals while scheduling such as taking whatever classes you want regardless of time or day of the week, stacking classes on certain days of the week, scheduling late classes so you can sleep in, or conversely early classes so the day is over quickly. Your schedule needs to closely align with your strengths, weaknesses, and priorities. I like to sleep late and dislike having to get ready to go to class multiple times in a day, because it was hard to motivate myself to leave once. I would usually have my classes start at 10:30 AM and have them stacked up so they're over by 3 PM or 4 PM.

I stand behind my process considering I never dropped a single class in five years of college. When sitting down to look at my degree audit or progress I had to see what sections I most needed to address. I would then go to the class registrar web page and sit with the list of need based classes to meet my requirements. A lot of students spend more than four years getting their bachelor's degree and you don't need to be one of them and certainly not if you're looking at student loans.

I would return to my dorm or apartment next with the list to find times, availability, and professors of the classes; to copy and paste the names and times onto Microsoft Word. Then I would look up the professor's names on ratemyprofessor.com to see how former students felt about the instructor. I would eliminate the instructors who got consistently poor reviews from the list. Would you buy a book from Amazon if it had a two-star rating (Amazon uses a rating scale with five-stars being the best)? I would be left with a pool of about 10-15 classes that I could choose to meet my requirements and the professor was not a jerk about projects or in general.

Essentially, my class search was like a game of "Guess Who?" with my constantly eliminating options to locate the elite few. With the final 10-15 classes I would look at the times and try to stack them on certain days of the week, preferably after 10 AM because I like going out and sleeping in the next morning. I learned good sleep was the best recipe to staying healthy in college, because a lot of kids get strung out on sleep. I also liked to give myself a day or two off during the week as well to work on projects both for class and personally.

Usually after all my stipulations I would have four or five classes left on my list. I may have to swallow my pride a bit and get up early one day out of the week or not have any days off to get the professors I want. But most times, I was able to line up my schedule as I liked and almost graduated in seven semesters from Penn State (a public school ivy league university). So I believe my system worked just fine; it took about four hours to research but was well worth it in the end because I was usually better rested and had easier classes than friends. This ultimately led to a higher GPA and several appointments to the dean's list.

Dorm Life

This is where you want to start your college residential career. Some colleges require a dorm residency freshman year anyway. Despite all the rules, crowded facilities, and hearing your neighbor hooking up through the walls, this is the place where you will gain the most success socially. Big risks yield big rewards, and dorm living is exactly that. It is the nice stepping-stone to apartment living, which you should certainly experience throughout your college career. You will still be living under a set of rules, but they are rather loose most places. Heaven forbid you get a tool of an RA on a power trip in your dorm.

You will be under the semi-supervision of a resident assistant who will be under the dorm coordinator, but realistically they're not babysitters and have their own life to worry about. Be darn sure that you do not tick these people off and get on their good side almost immediately. It will probably pay off later when you come back hammered, carrying a pizza, and wearing a football jersey of a school that is not your own. Not that it happened to in Mississippi; I'm just saying it may come in handy.

As stupid as some of the programs that directors run are, go to as many as possible. You never know when some good-looking girls are going to be there or your boys will be there and you'll have a blast. I was once at a family game night for five hours; when I got back I had seven friend requests on Facebook. Don't expect results like mine (not that I am the man), especially early on because this was during my last year of college and I over matched the experience of any other person in the room; it was simply fish in a barrel.

But do not tick off RA's as in the case of my freshman roommate who liked to get drunk and yell at RA's he knew were waiting out in the main lounge of the building. One particular night, this squirrelly kid who worked in the cafeteria and was an RA that was on duty. This little fella' used to always ask us if we wanted our receipt in the cafeteria because he worked at the register. Since you had a meal plan that was virtually unlimited you had no reason to ever want it; yet this guy always wanted to give it to us. He used to wear the Canadian Tuxedo get up with the sheepskin denim jacket and matching jeans. He was very uptight about everything and a stickler for the rules; certainly a kid we wanted to get messed up because it would have been the night of his life.

This night it was 1 AM and I was standing in my friend's room just watching him play a video game when my roommate stumbles in. He starts screaming "DO YOU WANT YOUR RECEIPT?" over and over to see if this kid will come. He knew he was getting in some dangerous territory, but this RA was one of these guys who was a tattle-tale and those are unwelcome at any age. He had gotten some of our other friends in trouble earlier in the year. After a while of screaming, this kid comes and stares down my roommate with his little squinty eyes and tells him to go to bed. To end the confrontation, my roommate calmly asks him in a whisper if he wanted his receipt, smiled, then went to our room for the night. It took every muscle in my body from not laughing right in the RA's face when my roommate did that.

If you are a freshman, they are probably going to throw you into a real dump where you'll have to walk a half mile to get to your car and have to adjust your heat by jamming a screw driver into the register. Nothing in the building will be comfortable because you will be surrounded by brick, concrete, and cold tile floors. You just make due as best as you can and keep reminding yourself that it will get better with each passing year. You really start learning that not everyone around you came from as good of an upbringing as you will regularly find messes in the hallways or bathrooms. Sometimes you may even have to pony up some cash to cover damages that you had nothing to do with.

One such example happened during my first semester at college in 2004. It had been a long week of getting assignments done and I wanted to sleep in until about noon. Most people had gone to University Park to go watch the Penn State vs. Iowa football game that day, which would turn out to be one of the worst games for a fan in the history of football with a 6-4 Iowa final. I woke up to the sound of knocking at my door, and when I jumped down to answer the door my feet were immediately submerged in water. Confused and groggy eyed, I walked to the door to answer it.

At the door were my friends on the other side to ask me about the water. I told them I knew nothing about it, and told them I would see them later after they got back from the game. Trying to figure out what happened I followed the water back to the source of where it was running from, the urinal in the bathroom across the hall. But because of a not perfectly level floor all the water ran into the four rooms on my side of the hall. I went knocking on the other doors to see if anyone was there, but only came up with my friend to help me out.

We walked to the maintenance office to find someone, but it was closed for the weekend. But we happened to stumble onto the cleaning people of residence hall, who were great, on our way back and they brought a bunch of mops and buckets. We spent all that morning going through rooms picking wet items up off the floor and mopping out all the water. It took a good few hours to get all off the water soaked up. The university did not pay for our damaged items citing that we were the victims of a prank and charged the rest of the wing.

I even had an encounter with the Phantom Shitters. We ran into one of these characters both years at Penn State-Altoona. Someone would take a random dump somewhere in the dorms and just leave it. Then people would get charged for its removal and carpet cleaning. The actual proper named used by staff was "Phantom Shitter," and this Phantom struck multiple times throughout the years.

After freshmen year we thought we had ridden ourselves of the Phantom. This pooper of the night was like Jack the Ripper (because I always pictured the phantom to be wearing a cape) striking with no consistency or motive during the night. But instead of dead prostitutes you just had a pile of excrement in a corner somewhere to be found. The Phantom struck again during sophomore year after a long layoff for summer, where he/she took their traveling act elsewhere. In all, we lost about $25 each from the Phantom for all I know has never been caught. They are probably in search of another opportunity to strike again in an office building near you.

Growing thick skin is essential because you will put up with a lot of junk. Often dealing with the communal shower foot disease haven will probably toughen you up. I was a personal victim of the Planter's wart. It took all summer to saw down those little guys in the shower.

Being forced to live closely with strangers will yield your true personality for the whole floor or dorm to see. You will need to have alligator blood because your roommate will want to bring girls back to the room, and you'll need to become comfy with a floor or a marginally comfortable lounge couch.

You have to be thankful that your roommate at least gave you the heads up before bringing a girl back to the dorms. The worst thing in the world is waking up in the middle of the act and not knowing what is going on because you're groggy and no one was there when you fell asleep. Once you come to and realize what is going on; it is too late you're wide-awake. It'll probably be be six degrees warmer than what it was when you fell asleep and there will always be one bad squeaky spring on your roommate's box spring. There will be some whispering and heavy breathing which is awful and very awkward for conversation the next day. Avoiding being trapped in this situation is the very reason why you give the heads up, and hope your roommate mutually does the same.

Don't worry what goes around comes around and he will have to do the same for you. There aren't many secrets in the dorms because most people have their doors wide open and there are thin walls. Get ready to have everyone know your business especially if you live in the farthest room down the hall from the entrance. Oh, and I definitely suggest leaving your door open at all times except the times when you don't want anyone in there. But even that won't stop them, so if you want any true peace and quiet hit up a study lounge.

A lot of your best stories will come from living in the close quarters of the dorm. A lot of times you will come up with a bunch of games to pass the time and there will be plenty of people there to join in. Just keeping active and social will provide for a great time in the dorms, and great networking for down the road. The kids who are miserable are the ones who spend all their time in their room alone and to themselves. If you get them to talk they will probably be pathetic, but it is their own fault. They should be out creating memories and opening up to have fun.

One night a friend and I and went to rent some movies a Movie Gallery at the bottom of the hill, just off campus. Luckily, we were able to find these pieces of cinema excellence and no one else had checked them out. Looking back on it, we were probably the only people to rent Rocky IV, Jingle All the Way, and Air Force One from that store in the previous five years. But it made for a terrific night when your university has been closed due to snow.

Now alcohol will definitely play a role in your dorm experience. Your friends probably won't care that it is 2:30 in the morning and will come knock on your door thinking you're still awake. But you would normally be just getting to sleep at that time on a Friday or Saturday night during the year, possibly even a Thursday night. But sometimes the party looms late and you get a wake-up call at closer to dawn.

I was once asleep at 5 AM when my door was kicked in by a friend from the third floor. I lived on the first floor so he traveled all the way down two flights of stairs wearing nothing but boxers to fight me. Not because he hated me or anything, but because he liked me and figured I'd be the type of guy who would want to brawl at 5 AM. He woke me up out of my sound sleep by putting me in a headlock and pulled me out of bed. Confused, I woke and managed to fight him off before one of our other buddies came down to retrieve him.

My freshman roommate and I did not lock our room on the premise that we did not own anything worth stealing. I had a three-year-old computer that crashed a lot and a stack of VHS tapes, so if I would have had anything stolen, they were probably doing me a favor. But you will probably own something that is worth keeping so I highly recommend locking your room. People getting stuff taken out of their room all the time, so be careful.

Use common sense when it comes to security in your rooms because people will most likely steal clothes, textbooks, IPods, cell phones if they are given the opportunity. No matter how well you think you know everyone in your building, people surprise you. You can't get too trusting because that will be the day when you're robbed.

You will have a lot of spare time in the dorms. We used to have poker tournament that were worth a few hundred dollars, fantasy sports, computer chair bowling with the recycling bins, pranks, and so much more. As far as pranks I prefer the old classic of the shaving cream in the sleeping person's hand, antiquing someone walking out of the showers, or stealing all the right shoes someone has. We once turned absolutely everything these kids owned upside-down one night.

One time a friend's prank on me. He was downstairs one Friday evening, and when he walked up he saw someone taking a shower and took their towel. He assumed that the towel was mine because it looked a lot like mine, so he took it and put it on my doorknob outside my room. He went back down to continue playing poker, but knew he was in trouble after a couple minutes when I called him from another building. Then about 15 minutes later a kid wearing the towel came down to fight him. This kid who was the mistaken victim of a prank was a huge douche who could not take a joke.

Another fun thing to do in the dorms is put random objects into the microwave and see what happens. My friends used to put all kinds of crazy things in there like handfuls of change, chip bags, a bar of soap, light bulbs, and a bunch of other stuff. You will have some crazy results such as chip bags will shrink up to the point where you can punch a hole in them and use them as a key chain; handful of change pretty just sparks like crazy; a bar of soap melts and turns into a pancake form that smells delicious; and light bulbs change colors until they get too hot and explode. An exploded light bulb is no joy to clean up, so make sure you take it out before that point.

Some less lethal objects to microwave include putting your names on a bunch of eggs and putting them in to see who lasts the longest and wins. Also putting a marshmallow Easter Peep is also hilarious; but I will leave that for you to enjoy. But putting things in the microwave is only a small portion of the purpose of a microwave and what it can do. I often made triple layer nachos in the microwave to enjoy as I sit back and watch some Monday Night Football with the boys, but this was one of the few edible items that went in. Obviously, I take no responsibility if you burn your place to the ground after trying the stunts mentioned in this book.

You may admire the independent living of friends in the apartments you are going to visit, but they are missing the convenience of having an entire campus of students there to talk to. During your time as freshman you will have to come up with schemes to get away with drinking, gambling, and other activities that are frowned upon. Most RA's do not care as long as you're not a jerk about it, and just warn you to keep it down because they did the same thing the year before. But they get free housing this year to act as a glorified adviser and babysitter; so the only real person to worry about is the hall director and their routine maintenance checks.

One such story of bad luck drinking in the dorms leads back to a friend of mine. During our freshmen year he really didn't drink at all, but one night we were up having a few drinks up in our friend's room. I ended up taking off after a while, but my buddy that lived down the hall kept going and didn't know his limits. He ended up getting pretty tanked and feeling sick so he returned to his room. For whatever reason he left his room to go throw up in the communal bathroom, which is a big no-no because if an RA on rounds or a hall director catch you they have to call campus police and report it. If he would have been smart enough to stay in his room to throw up in his trash can and deal with it later he would have made it through the night.

What is important to know is that the residence life cannot open anything in your room (every place I've been) to check for alcohol. As long as there are no clues to the presence of alcohol such as empty cans or the box it came in, they will never know when they come in for room checks. As long as you don't slip up by having the room way too loud some night, get an underage in the dorm, or leave cans and bottles all over the place you should never get in trouble. It has been rare that I have ever heard anyone get in trouble for underage possession of alcohol in the dorms. Usually no one is that dumb.

They say the checks are for maintenance, but it is to size you up and get a good idea what is going on. I once got a fire hazard warning for a coffee pot I did not own; I mean I don't even drink nor enjoy coffee so they obviously don't root deeper to see what you really have. The good thing about these fire alarms is people come out of the woodwork. You will see people you didn't know lived in your dorms, and girls you didn't know existed because they are always in their rooms. It is a bittersweet situation, use the fire alarm as a chance to chat it up and make plans.

With the dorms you will need to have a meal plan at the cafeteria. No matter how good the cafeteria is you will get sick of it eventually, because eating there constantly is like eating anywhere all the time. Even if you said Burger King was your favorite restaurant in the world, eventually you will get tired of eating chicken nuggets and

Whoppers if forced to go there every meal. The cafeteria will be the same way, some days will be terrific and other will be god-awful.

Most schools have a meal plan and then a separate account for bonus bucks or whatever they want to call them for other restaurants on or around campus. Do not use all these bonus bucks at once, and for the love of all things holy, don't take a girl out on a date to a place on campus and use bonus bucks. You will not look smooth, but cheap because your parents probably paid for your meal plan. Spread out the dollars throughout the semester so you can keep your sanity. You don't want to be trapped into eating cafeteria food for the last two months straight of the semester. A lot of campuses will have some contract with a chain restaurant that you can use bonus bucks with, which is always a nice perk.

Conversely, you have idiots that have a car and do not like the cafeteria who go off campus all the time to restaurants. These guys spend tons of money after already dropping $1,000 for the meal plan for the semester started. I've never understood the people who always go off campus all the time for food. If I've already paid for a meal, I can stomach it even if it isn't my favorite over paying another $6 for a combo meal.

First thing to know is that the homemade pizza that a lot of school make will be sub-par but manageable; however most of the meat is what I call Scooby Doo, or mystery meat. It is a complete mystery to me what kind of meat you will be eating in those burgers or quesadillas. I've literally made it through sandwiches and wraps not knowing what type of meat I just consumed. Make it interesting by putting money on what kind of meat it is then ask someone working. You don't want a sandwich full of S.D. because it is low quality stuff. But you will need to stomach it and realize that there will be better days ahead.

People will always look forward to certain days like homemade fried chicken day, chicken fillet days, and other inventions of the cafeteria crew to keep them sane and students from wanting to murder them. If students hear of these days or see the option, game over they are going to that line and you better saddle up for a 20 minute wait to get the only non-turd sandwich on the menu.

I recall such days at my first college, Penn State-Altoona. The air was always full of passion when two days arose on the monthly menu, because they were rare, possibly only offered once every two weeks. Normally, we got the same options every day: sub-par pizza, deli sandwiches, grilled/fried chicken sandwiches, mediocre burgers, salad bar, pasta, soups, and a random entrée. This may sound terrific, but when you're eating there twice a day for about 200 days a year it gets old. Popcorn chicken day was an exciting time, but nothing compared to the next day I will throw out.

Chicken Quesadilla Day was the most important Wednesday of the month for those students who lived on campus and for some of those who lived off campus as well. People would order as many as six or seven of these heavenly creations of chicken and cheese, which was hell for whoever was cooking them. Try to picture the New York Stock Exchange exploding with buyers.

It was like standing over a hot grill, a never-ending line of people ordering three days worth of food, all day on Chicken Quesadilla Day. People would be calling others in the cafeteria to save them a spot in line or pick them up a few, as if World Series tickets were going on sale. For the sake of the cafeteria, they probably should have had quesadilla day more than once a month to take some of the edge off.

Lastly, Stir Fry day was a favorite of the campus. There were plenty of meat and vegetable options to throw with your rice and make for a good hearty meal. Often I would get a couple of bowls and go sit and watch TV like a fat cat for the rest of the evening. The cafeteria food at Penn State-Altoona was delicious; it was much better than Southern Miss, which has a cafeteria three times the size.

Roommates

Getting roommates, particularly random roommates, is like spinning the big wheel on the *Price is Right*, it is tough to gauge what you're going to get. You definitely want someone with personality who is not always in the room, because it sucks when you come back and they are always there. Then you have the random people that just use your stuff like it is their own eating food, wearing clothes, and taking plates as they please with no intention of ever giving you anything in return. It takes all your will not to beat their legs with a hammer one night while they're sleeping.

It is hard to tell anything about anyone from just meeting them or being friends with them. Living with someone is when you find the real dirt about them; like their love of Full House or wearing only tighty-whities eating a can of ravioli when they're just sitting around. Yes, they may make you want to vomit from time to time because they never do their laundry, but these off the wall people will probably be the source of much laughter. Also keep in mind, that you are probably no prize to live with either.

I have had seven roommates in my five years of college. I kept in touch with all of them. I don't know if it is because I'm easy to live with, but I'm not overly critical about the way my roommate would like to live. I've lived with kids who smoke pot, drink, are of a different race, from different economical levels, from different regions, and so many other differences, but I have found a way to relate. I think being able to roll with the punches is the key to survival as you get new roommates.

I had friends who were rarely able to find common ground with their new roommates because of petty differences. I've heard about fights over a can of soup, bottle of beer, what movie to watch, and a host of other stupid reasons, which helps feeds into a poor relationship with your roommate. People don't see that their little rituals and habits are just as annoying as their roommate's. You need to be flexible about the little things that you don't agree with, and don't sweat the small stuff as they say. Keep your eye on the big picture.

Sometimes it easier to have a random roommate assigned to you rather than go with someone you know, especially if you don't know them that well. I've heard about so many times where people think that moving in together will be a match made in heaven, but it turns out a nightmare. One such instance was a group of girls that lived down the hall from my apartment as a junior in State College. I knew two of the girls and heard drastically different stories from both of them, so it is hard to know who to trust. They were great friends moving into their apartment, but they quickly found reasons to fight and not spend the night in their apartment that they pay over $400 a month for. They fought over petty things like who gets the last handful of chips or who does the dishes. The fights always grew into something larger, and it almost destroyed their friendship.

Personally, the things that annoyed me more than anything was just little oversights. I've had multiple roommates who don't put the seat up when they pee and it ends up all over the seat. When I come back doing the "Texas Two-Step" from Taco Bell the last thing I want to do is take the time to clean off someone's dried urine from the seat. Also I was a big stickler for getting the dishes done because they would start to smell over time and we would run out of certain utensils. Lastly, I couldn't stand when others ate my food without my permission because I didn't have a car to go get groceries.

I'm never the kind to get nervous often and certainly never let it show on the outside. After being through many tough sports games, being on an intensely difficult academic track, and planning many events, pressure is just the way of life that none of us can avoid. Moving into college was supposed to be just another day for me, but I'll admit I was nervous whenever I passed the Altoona in 21 miles sign on my way to moving in my freshman year. Here I was a small town kid moving into a dorm with a kid I only knew was from the Pittsburgh area.

Just handling the academic workload, making friends, and playing intramural sports was my only real concern coming into college. When I got to Altoona that fateful day, it was unbearably hot with the temperature somewhere in the 90's, which is rare for this far north. I had one of the late move-in times because I was coming from over three hours away, and once I finally moved in it was six hours after my roommate had come in. Lugging in my first boxes full of essentials I saw all of his stuff moved in to the right side of the room. I've never been one to pack a bunch of stuff for a move, not compared to the few U-Hauls I saw outside of a dorm. This amazed me because a dorm is so small that it is nearly impossible to squeeze a U-Haul of items in.

After a short while, I finally met my roommate and we seemed like a good match on paper seeing he was class president and had interest in playing for the baseball team in Altoona, just as I had. Neither of us ended up playing baseball, but we got a long fairly well throughout the year with only a few clashes. This happens a lot with freshmen roommates because they've had their own room, with more space for the past few years and have generally had it their way. So moving in with a stranger into tighter quarters, tempers will brew in freshmen. Occasionally, you'll have shouting matches, and perhaps even request room assignment switches to avoid one another. But my freshman roommate was a great guy and we're still good friends to this day.

The people who tend to fight do it with more than one roommate because they refuse to make the adjustments needed to deal with living with someone new. It isn't a dictatorship; it is a democracy where you just try to get the important understandings to you in your favor. You can't have it your way anywhere but Burger King, and even that is usually messed up in some fashion. You'd be surprised how much you improve in your life when you're willing to make adjustments.

During your freshmen year, you start to meet people and develop your group of close friends. This is usually a pretty large group of people, since it is tough to know who your good friends are after only eight months of living with one another. But living in the crowded freshmen dorms will give you the opportunity to see who a person really is 10 times faster than you would if they were a commuter or living in an apartment.

The person who I originally signed up to live with as a sophomore had to bail from our contract. He had to attend a different campus to meet his requirements to get into his major. This put me behind the ball with only a couple of options to choose from. Most people had already signed up to live with someone like I had. This meant I had to spend a lot of time finding out who still needed a roommate and not be shy about it.

After consideration I was down to my friends (we'll call them Pat and Nick). I knew Pat (or C.P.) very well because he was a kid who would go out of his way to do whatever you needed to get done. If you were a good guy to him, he was great to you and would help out in any way to make sure there were no problems. Not a lot of people, particularly girls, really got to know him very well and were often crept out by him. He had an odd personality and was very straightforward; an attribute I enjoy, but not all people do.

On the other hand, I had Nick who I had met later in my freshman year. At first I didn't really like Nick when we played basketball against one another. He sort of had a combative personality, and a certain toughness to him that I did not like. But over time we found an understanding and later on in college he would become one of my best friends. In fact, we were in the same major and had plenty of classes together. We had been co-hosts on a radio show that we established and were hosts of for two years.

I leaned towards living with Pat because of my stronger familiarity with him. I knew what I was getting into, and I've always been one to calculate the odds. You would know this if you ever went shopping with me because I take forever price comparing products and measuring what I will and will not eat. So heading into sophomore year I would be moving in Pat into the nicest dorms on campus.

Pat and I moved in early our sophomore year because we were e-mailed an offer to be paid to help others move into the dorms. So he worked in a parking lot, and I kept track of the list of freshmen moving in another lot so not too many people were overwhelming the freshmen lots. But once we got settled into our place it was a pretty relaxing year in our suite style apartment. I was sharing a bathroom with my freshman year roommate and his roommate. We had a naturally tight bond with one another upon moving in.

During our sophomore year, there were very few arguments amongst the four of us in the dorm. We all had our own weekly schedules and really only hung out during the weekends in another's rooms. We also had a good collection of our close friends that had moved up to the apartments up on the hill. We spent a great deal of time at our friends' apartment complex, and in many ways it was my second home that year. Going out is really where the true bonds happened between my roommates and the guys I was visiting.

When it came time to move to Penn State-University Park, I had a great nucleus of friends to choose from. We took our time and toured a lot of apartment complexes to make sure we found one that was a great location for social life, and had good proximity to class, and plenty of floor space for four guys. As time passes, it becomes easier to know what personalities you live with best, and you find out a lot about yourself.

It is necessary to just put yourself out there and allow people to know the real you. When you live with people it is going to come out anyway. They'll see you at your best and at your worst. During your college years, you'll spend more time with roommates than with your own our own family. It's worth taking the time to work on getting along well with the people you live with.

Friends

Many universities have a lot of clubs and groups that will mesh with your interests. You need to get involved in clubs, organizations, and intramurals to not only develop socially, but professionally. You do not want to get in over your head too deep, because I had some friends who have been overwhelmed by obligations from clubs on top of trying to do class work. I knew athletes at Penn State who had a hard enough time as it was just playing their sport and getting their academics done. Major college sports are a business and there are high bars set athletically, but you have to take care of business in the classroom too. This great demand of your energy does not leave much time for family and friends.

In college, I had friends of all different races, nationalities, political views, religions, and lifestyle choices. Seeing how other people who aren't really like you live helps develop the type of person you are and develops the type of person you will become. Being open to meeting all kinds of different people is essential to understanding where those types of people come from.

As a freshman you will be meeting so many people all the time that it will be hard to remember names and the faces that go with them. Sometimes, you'll have to embarrassingly ask someone what their name is again. You know you hate it when people don't remember your name, so you can understand how they feel. But this is common, and you probably won't even be friends with half the people you meet as a freshman. But it is OK; you will probably cross paths with these people later on down the road and may kindle a friendship or have an awkward "hi" going to class. I knew one kid who used to do the fake gunpoint thing at me for two years and to this day I can't remember how I know him.

Over time you will develop deeper relationships with them because you will go through a lot of trials and tribulations with them. You will help people out and you will be saved from time to time when tough times arise. The friends who you go through crazy times with are the ones you'll still be talking to when you're 60. As you develop socially, it will be easier to put your neck out there to help someone else in need. Don't be afraid to ask your best friends for help either because they maybe going through the same problems.

I have seen dorks, creeps, and sheltered kids turn into some of the coolest kids I know. I, in fact, was a shy skinny kid when I got to college who did not know a party from his right pinky. Sitting around and talking deep into the night with my friends were some of the best nights of my life. Those are the things I will really remember, and not some physics equation I learned as a sophomore. College is more about life lessons than it is about lessons in the classroom. You'll fail a lot, but it is how you respond to those failures that will define you.

I think I definitely grew more socially than I ever came close to academically. Don't get me I did well graduating from Penn State with a 3.31 and Southern Miss with a 3.72, but I certainly am not the same person leaving as I was coming in. My friends that I made influenced me for the better and made me take bigger risks than I would have ever considered in high school. Some decisions I made were bad, but most of them I wouldn't take back for a million dollars. Alright maybe a million, but not for $175.50 (a fine my buddy got for public urination). These risks give you confidence that you will need later on in college and in life.

Taking these risks mean staying out until dawn, skipping a class, being there for a friend when it might not be convenient for you, talking to the girl who may be out of your league, and so many more examples. However, don't get desperate and make really stupid decisions, but a dumb risky move is OK from time to time. Having the confidence to go against your normal grain and take a look at the bigger picture will develop you as a person and give you a new perspective on life. Throwing parties and not charging guests, but expecting the same from them is a big risk and a big reward, but so worth it.

I remember throwing one of many of our parties and waking up the next morning with cups all over the ground four floors below my balcony. Just waking up with your hair all jacked up and people you don't know sleeping on your floor, while you stumble over them to get some fresh air is a rare experience. Red solo cups, beer cans, bottles, 40's, sun glasses, old cigars were to be found all over the parking lot below our place after a party, so I knew people had a good time. At the time, I groaned knowing I would have to clean up all this junk, but now I really miss those days because they were a blast.

The balcony at my apartment of three years was kind of a special place because it was home to a lot of memories. There were a lot of fights, heart-to-heart talks, drunken chats, and time to relax out in the sun on a nice summer evening. Just getting up and being away from all your work, your computer, and where people can bother you can be so soothing. That balcony was our safe zone where you were able to take a breather from the fast-paced life of a college student.

When parties started getting going at our place the balcony was often the scene of friends smoking pot and drinking 40's. On one particular occasion a friend of ours poured a shot of Everclear on the railing of the balcony and proceeded to light it. We looked on in a panic for any police officers, but then once we saw that the foot and a half flames were not going to spread we all had a pretty good laugh.

The hardest days of college are the first ones when everyone you know is left at home or spread out at other colleges. You have your back against the wall and you are the bottom of the totem pole socially. Freshmen guys are even below freshmen girls, because we're not even wanted at fraternity houses unless we want to rush to their house. Most of the guys I knew who rushed had type A personalities or simply had a hard time making friends and needed an organization as a sort of crutch.

It just seemed like the clubhouse you had when you were a kid and only certain people were in the club, and outsiders were looked down upon. But I understand why those guys get so close going through all of the ritual and rush activities together is like any team or group forming a bond with one another.

When I first joined Facebook back in 2004, I was skeptical about what it could do for me. It just seemed like I was creating another profile on a random site that I would never use, because this was before a photo album, events, or any of the applications Facebook has today. Coming into college I would have never expected such an innovation to develop, I would simply go on forgetting about people and the important dates in my life. But despite this I find there is a great deal of ridiculousness to many of the applications used on Facebook just years after I became a member. It has come a long way and has made quite a bit of money but I think the site has become a victim of its own growth.

I will share one of the best times I ever had with my friends and it was during my sophomore year while still at Penn State-Altoona. It was 2005, and I had season tickets to a football team that was a Top 25 program during that season. It was the biggest home game of the year with the Ohio State Buckeyes coming into town that Saturday night and a national telecast on ESPN. We would leave Friday night to get up to State College and go to College Gameday which was broadcasting outside of the basketball arena.

We left on a chilly Friday afternoon for State College, about a 45-minute drive from our campus. With me were some of my best friends driving in a Silver Bullet mini-van (Dodge Caravan). We loaded up on supplies getting a grill, food, and tailgating tent (which we later found out they didn't ring up but we didn't think Wal-Mart would miss the $40 tent once we figured it out). When we got to town we were met by heavy traffic, which is customary the day before a Penn State football game. People come from Virginia, Maryland, New Jersey, New York, Washington D.C., and all parts of Pennsylvania to make Beaver Stadium one of the largest cities in the state on game day.

This was the first week of the tent city outside Beaver Stadium named Paternoville, after legendary Penn State head coach Joe Paterno. The students had been camped outside the gate with their ticket for a chance to sit front row for the biggest game in program history in over five years. There was a high degree of intensity and anticipation in the air when we rolled into Happy Valley that Friday evening. The camp was so crowded and loud that it took up everything from the gates to the road (about 75 yards) and they beat on recycling bins all night to Penn State fight songs. I don't think anyone slept the night before the game. I could hear the drum beats a 1/2 mile from where it was being played even at 4 AM.

We spent much of our time in traffic with the van doors open on both sides going down the road blasting Led Zeppelin's best hits as we went. All four of us were like little kids waiting on Christmas Eve for a present still yet unknown. We finally got to our parking spot, and set up our tailgate tent as darkness was setting on the valley. Soon there after a man in an orange vest came down to tell us we needed to pack everything up and leave the area. But as my one friend says, "Only do something when someone asks twice." So we stayed in the spot and spent the night in the van.

It was an uncomfortable night because we were all jammed in the Silver Bullet trying to sleep. I had my feet hanging out the back of the van, while the others slept in uncomfortable seats in other parts of the van. During the night a cold front bringing rain came into the area and rained on us. But we only woke up when a car came in at 2 AM shining its bright lights in at us; that is when we noticed the entire lower half of our bodies be soaked and cold. Me, being the grump I am when someone wakes me up got up and peed on the car that woke us up after its owners had left. I was able to curl back in the van and get some much-needed uncomfortable hours of sleep.

The next morning we woke up to people talking in our tailgating tent; it just so happened that we were staying next to a group of Ohio State alumni who slept in their car (the one I didn't pee on) much like we did. We told them that it was a shame that they drove this far to see their team lose. After some initial tension we gathered all the food we had and threw it on the grill because we knew we had to get in line as soon as possible.

I walked up to where College Gameday was shooting and were able to get in the pit directly behind the stage. I was one of those guys you saw pointing at the camera and nearly going deaf from my buddy screaming in my ear. This is something I feel all college students should experience once, because the show is legendary and you won't always get a chance to experience it. It was the first time Gameday had been there since 1999 and Penn State's match-up with Arizona to kickoff the season. Right after that was over we went over to get in line at the student entrance at noon.

The game didn't kick off until 8 PM, but there were still over 1,000 people in front of us at line. Over time the line got longer and longer and expanded the some 75 yards all the way back to the road. It was so tight I was smashed against my friends for a good hour and a half before they opened the gates 90 minutes before kicked off. After that it was a strong push to the front behind our van driver who is about 6'2" and 240 pounds and extremely aggressive.

We got to our seats to enjoy what could have been the loudest game ever on ESPN and most certainly the loudest in stadium history. The sound waves were so strong that rows of people would collapse from the seats they were standing on. On a normal game day, it wasn't unusual for a row of people to fall to the ground in unison, but for 5-7 rows to go down is something I've never seen before or after. When the game ended and Penn State won 17-10 we were hugging one another on the ground and high fiving we've never met before in our lives.

We rushed the field and got on for a short while, before riot police came out to shoo the students off the field. My friends and I got separated but were instructed to meet back at the Silver Bullet. This was a real treat after such a monstrous game. It definitely stands as one of the landmark times in my friendship with these three guys and a weekend I will always remember.

Apartment Life

When you move into an apartment you really take your independence from your parents a step further. You will now have to cook, clean, handle bills, go grocery shopping on a larger scale, and pay your rent; all a major leap forward. But not you have a very loose set of rules, answering only to your rental agency and the police. It makes you really feel like an adult no longer having to go to the cafeteria to eat.

I lived in the same apartment for a little over two years in State College and the location was terrific, only about a block and a half off campus and a 15 minute walk from my classes. I had to share a room with a high school friend, and the apartment with two other guys I knew from Penn State-Altoona. Looking for the apartment was a good experience because taking tours with these guys was a blast. That laid back attitude I think jolted a lot of the truths about the buildings loose from the lady taking us around. We went to four buildings before we decided on our place, which we lived in from August of 2006 to August of 2009.

Finding Your Bachelor Pad

The first step is finding the apartment that you want to live in. Depending on where you go to school this can be a major challenge in itself. Some housing is only designated for students, while others are for professionals and graduate students so not everything is available to you. You need to understand what is important to you when picking out your place. Do they allow pets? Do you want to drive to class or walk? Do you want your own room or can you share? Do you like it quiet or do you enjoy the nightlife? How much are you willing to pay per month? What are the utilities? These are just a few of the questions that will need to be addressed when picking out your place.

There are a lot of people who like to live close to campus and have all the businesses, bars, and stores right there for them. They will most likely have very little square footage as compared to friends who live farther away from campus and may pay the same. But for them it is a hassle to get in their car or hop in a bus to waste time commuting to campus, which you walk to. This will also hinder their nightlife plans because they will need a designated driver, follow a bus schedule, or crash on someone's couch. Those that lived close get to go home to their own bed that night.

Each college town will have a number of agencies you can go through to find a place to live the next semester or year. If you only need the place for a semester and are not particular about much, a sub-lease is probably for you. The best route I have found is CraigsList by a wide margin. As long as you don't move in with a bunch of slobs or asses you'll be fine to get done whatever you need to. But most people will sign a full year's lease, because six month and school-year (9 ½ month) leases are nearly impossible to find. If you do discover a lease that only covers the school year, it will be more expensive because the inconvenience you cause the rental agency. Rental companies bet that you're willing to pay for the extra few months to have the place throughout the school year. That's why I always called their bluff by living in the place if I was paying for it, even if school was out.

Make sure you tour your place before agreeing to sign to the lease so you get an idea if it comes close to matching what you want out of a place. You will want to take into account size, condition, age of appliances, location, parking, utilities, and move-in dates, as well as other desires you may have. A lot of these can be negotiated as well, as the company loves guarantee and money. Make sure you ask a bunch of questions so you make the company really work to get you to agree you renting the place. But don't bite at the first place you look at, go to a few others just to compare and contrast styles and costs so you know where you stand.

I took a tour of one place that looked like something out of a crime scene. There were kids just lying around and they obviously smoked weed because the place reeked of it. The apartment was a lot smaller than we thought; even though the price was extremely cheap we passed. We toured five places altogether before we discovered where we wanted to live, but we were happy with our decision and had an enjoyable experience for the most part. Except for maintenance always showing up at 8 AM to do painting or any other kind of work, the staff was great. Don't be afraid to call maintenance because it's better to have it fixed now than have it come out of your deposit.

You will be confronted with the choice of furnished vs. unfurnished apartments when you are searching for your place. "Furnished" means that all the grunt work out of moving in, but you have to remember that the items you are living with are not yours and you need to be careful. In contrast, the unfurnished apartment makes you do all this extra work of getting a U-Haul or truck to move in all your furniture, but you get to put your stamp of personality in the apartment. Also, all that furniture is yours and you don't own anyone inflated costs if it breaks. I would recommend a furnished place if you plan on being there for two or less years. They will cost a little more (typically 10-20% more per month), but will be worth it. The impending doom that is moving furniture and finding vehicles does loom large in your mind.

Getting a furnished apartment will take a lot of headaches out, even if it does cost you an extra per month and you risk losing your deposit if they are damaged. Most of the furnished furniture is of low quality because the rental company does not want to risk higher end furniture to college age kids who throw parties. I can't really blame them because I have seen some jacked up couches, walls, dressers, beds, and kitchen counters in my day. There are a lot of people who do not care about what happens to their place after they leave, they're more than willing to lose their deposit money over having a good time. Somehow my bed frame ended up four floors down in the parking lot one morning after a party. How can I be judgmental of the quality of furniture they choose to put in there?

The dreaded checklist of damages and making sure you don't get screwed

When you move in they will give you a checklist of items to check throughout the apartment and a deadline in which to return it by. Go around and actually check everything on the list because the company has the list as well and will charge you with any damages, even if you did not do the damage. The company also has heavily inflated costs to every crappy item that they have furnished the apartment with. On top of paying for the item, you have to pay for the time the work is done, which must be done at an alarming $100 an hour.

We got charged $30 to re-glue a handle on a mirror. To put this insanity in perspective, I once had my rear view mirror fall off while driving at an internship I had in Florida. It cost me less money to have guys drive out, glue the mirror back on and account for their time than it did to re-glue a small handle on my bathroom mirror.

Put items on the list of being damaged even if there is just a little wear and tear so you can refer to it when you move out. This will save you money, and will certainly cut down on the costs of paying for the workers. Having a set of tools around to make minor repairs is also a great thing to have around, because you never know when you'll need them. I recommend the trio of WD-40, duct tape, and an adjustable wrench. You can make a bunch of minor repairs and make a trip to a Lowe's or Home Depot to pick up some spare parts at a highly discounted price instead of paying for the company to replace it. Remember, the rental people must be related to the textbook people who all graduated with a Bachelor of Science Degree in Thievery.

Give yourself an extra day at the end of your lease to clean and repair anything that is needed. The rental company will find any excuse to keep your deposit so don't give them one. At least make furniture and the apartment clean and passable to the naked eye. Make it the problem of the next people moving in to discover problems and write it on their check-in damages sheet for the company to fix. That way everyone wins.

My freshmen roommate lived in a house that looks like a place they would shoot a "Saw" movie in at the end of Penn State's notorious East Beaver Avenue. There was a problem with asbestos in the basement of the house, which I took a tour of before knowing of the airborne killer. The rest of the house pretty much resembled what you would expect from a house lived in by squatters. Although the location was great, only blocks from bars and campus and a big enough place for parties; it looked like it could go up in flames at any moment. It had extremely old appliances and was made of old wood, and I'm pretty sure there had to have been ghosts living there as well.

What do you honestly need for an apartment?

You will need to get necessary items for your apartment, and I will address much of that in the shopping chapter of the book. But it is important to know that you don't need to drop as much bank as you would think to make this empty apartment a home. Most of my friends have posters and promotional items they got for free lining their walls and giving the place a personality. There is so much free stuff hanging around college campuses put out by marketing departments that it isn't really necessary to spend much money to decorate a place.

Some items that are probably pretty essential for a college apartment are a vacuum cleaner, mop and bucket, cleaning supplies, speakers, and a beer pong table -- the rest is for show. Beer pong is a staple of college living, it doesn't matter who you are. The game is so popular that it must be present in every college household, much like the Nintendo of old or the random Jimi Hendrix or Bob Marley poster today.

You watch all that Home and Garden television and they talk about all these fancy decorations and great set ups. You don't need all that crap, because it is an extraordinary waste of money (money you don't have) to try to give your apartment a theme. I have been to people's places and they have wasted hundreds of dollars on items that they probably will throw away at the end of the year. As fancy as I ever got was having my two cacti I've grown since age 11 and putting them on the window ledge above my bed. Even the cacti were a bad idea in my apartment because my Old Man cactus was lit on fire twice and now that the hair has grown back stronger it looks like a certain part of the male anatomy.

If you want to have girls come over that don't work with the environmental protection agency, you should clean at least every other week. This includes vacuuming, mopping, cleaning out the fridge, dishes, dusting, bathrooms, the works. We learned the hard way because our carpet started reeking of moisture, the dishes would pile up, the kitchen floor developed a sticky layer and then a dirty layer on top, and science projects peered out from the fridge. Also the counters needed cleaned regularly because one roommate loved to make food that involved lots of spaghetti sauce. We always had people over that added to the mess that had accumulated over time.

The jobs need to be rotated because no one wants to constantly be stuck doing dishes or cleaning the bathroom. Those are the awful weeks, but you should only have to put up with that every other week tops. You have to agree upon some sort of system to getting the cleaning done, because you don't want to end up like us spending nine hours right before we move out cleaning off messes that could have been addressed in 90 seconds once a month throughout our stay. Also you don't want people bringing gas masks when they come over to your place.

Standard Apartment Fights

The main fights that will occur in an apartment usually have to deal with cleaning or some sort of bedroom etiquette problem. The cleaning problem occurs when they make a mess and don't clean it up for days at a time or don't do the chores they are supposed to. Usually somebody is the mother of the apartment, and is the first to confront the person who is slacking and a small fight ensues, much to delight of the other roommates who look on. Eventually somebody cleans up the mess and the grudge ends.

The bedroom etiquette is a little bit trickier because of moving into a room together. Living in an apartment you expect some sort of independence that you do not receive in the dorms, but sharing a room is much like living in a dorm. There have to be sacrifices made and you have to negotiate with one another about problems that are occurring.

I'm a night owl who will sometimes stay up until 2 or 3 in the morning when my roommate had early classes and I usually keep the blinds mostly shut which annoyed him for some reason. In contrast, things he did that annoyed me was standing right next to my bed early in the morning spraying Axe on himself and all over the room. He kept the TV on at night that was incredibly bright and I need darkness and quiet to sleep. But we both remained calm knowing we occasionally ticked one another off and looked past those flaws.

One particular fight that rears its ugly head is eating someone else's food. In my apartment, much like any college apartment, everyone's food is off-limits unless asked for. Going into the fridge and eating someone's leftovers from a meal or just using a bunch of their stuff without paying or asking is a mortal sin. My roommate came home after the bars one night and my high school friend had eaten his last piece of Papa John's pizza. My roommate responded with instant rage by ripping the breakfast bar in our kitchen from its attachable base. Needless to say that came out of all of our deposit.

The last main cause of fights is not paying someone for utilities. This is something that needs to be nipped in the bud as soon as the check comes because the last thing you need to do is tick off the utility company. Everyone needs to contribute their part of the payment when the check comes. Most apartment companies pay for most, if not all, of the utilities so they are not overwhelming.

Those who cannot get past petty differences that cause fights in an apartment are doomed for the dreaded breakup. This means the remaining roommates have to find someone to replace the person who bails. Then the person who bails has to find a group moving into an apartment and join them. It is really just a big hassle for everyone involved. So it is a great idea not to sweat the small stuff and get past it all to living with one another.

Going Shopping for Food and Style for Your Place

You will be solicited to get credit cards and open bank accounts at the beginning of your freshmen year and every school year afterwards. If you don't already have a checking and a savings account open one up. In fact through your college career I would recommend having two accounts from different banks so it is not all stashed in one place. The last thing you need to do is to get drunk with your debit card and wake up the next morning with a $250 charge on it from tequila shots. Not that I know anyone that has done that.

It will be useful to have a credit card or two to build credit, because one day you will need to have a good history to buy a house or a car. So I recommend a credit card or two and 1-2 banks to open accounts at so you can build a history in case you need to take out a loan years later. But pay your bill in full and on time. Nothing is dumber than paying credit card interest. But now that we've talking about saving on some of your costs let's explore spending it.

Let's take a look at an approach to shopping while in college. It is important to make your apartment comfortable despite the high probability that you won't have any money. But others should not think you are a creep whenever they come over to your place. I was skeptical when my roommates bought a "Brokeback Mountain" movie poster and put it prominently in our apartment for all to see. My roommates got the poster because people complained about our walls being bare. They called it a Soviet run unit because of the plain white bare walls and the fact that Russians owned our building. Luckily, the place was furnished or it would have been extraordinarily boring.

Your apartment needs to express your style and be welcoming to those who come over. Hit up some yard sales or garage sales to find something your style and deck out the place, but don't make it a junkyard. I've seen such places and they're awful. Make it fun and livable.

You'll have plenty of time to buy real furniture when you are a working professional and aren't having 20 people over every Thursday for an impromptu party. The new chairs will most definitely end up with spilled drinks all over them, and you'll be too lazy to clean them when you have an eight-page paper due on macroeconomics the next day. You're still learning to be on your own, so anything more than cheap foldout camping chairs is probably a little too much effort.

Most girls I know spend way too much money to get items for their apartment so they look stylish and classy. This is achieved, but at a higher cost than is necessary. It isn't like Home and Garden network are going to kick down the door to take a tour of their place. My roommates and I got all of our kitchen utensils and plates from flea markets and from hand-me-downs from other friends and family members. I do not need classy square plates, I can deal with the plates that look like they were stolen from the Brady Bunch prop storage facility is just fine with me. My plates had an ugly green stripe and a useless tiny pumpkin blazed on the plate. I got them because a guy was giving them away for free at a flea market so he could go home.

You will have pretty much everything you need already from living in the dorms to survive apartment living. There is no reason to get fancy spending money outside of a few decorations, such as a cheesy group photo you blew up and framed or a "Brokeback Mountain" poster that your roommates purchased. Even a random flag is all right to hang up and saves money; your apartment doesn't need to look like a sports bar. I'm pretty sure if you have girls and booze in the same place people will want to come over.

Some items I will recommend getting are an air freshener, preferably one of those one with all the goofy little sticks coming out of it or the cone air fresheners. Those are cheap, but not overpowering like the Glades plug-ins you get. Your place will eventually either smell like feet or beer and no girl wants to walk into that environment. So it is necessary to at least give off the appearance of cleanliness via the nose, because even if there is a mess in the apartment there is no smell to substantiate how long it has been there. As soon as the stench rears its ugly head, people will not want to hang out anymore. So make sure you keep the windows open when the weather is nice and buy a fan to circulate air and also talk into to make funny voices like you're Darth Vader. In addition, do not buy the spray can stuff because that only momentarily solves the stench problem. Do not even put it in the bathroom; it just raises a red flag that you had the bean burrito at Taco Bell earlier.

Buying one of those covers that you can put over a plate before it goes in the microwave is important. It is only a matter of time before you blow something up in the microwave like a plate of pasta sauce and create a great mess. Putting a bowl of hot water in the microwave and trying to vapor the dried and burnt food from the ceiling can only address this. Also getting the cover will cost less than buying plastic wrap over time.

Saving money should be your main focus so always scour the clearance racks at places like Wal-Mart and Target because outside of flea markets that is where we got the rest of our essentials. Most of the stuff was 75% off because we really didn't care about design so much as purpose of the item. You're not rolling in the dough yet, so no reason to lie to everybody with a fancy place when you're searching for loose change in the couch so you can get something off the $1 menu.

You will have a limited budget to buy food. A game my brother-in-law used to play is called "Nothing but Store Brand" where we were not allowed to buy anything but store brand products. This is kind of an extreme method, but here are some highly recommended hints that I learned in years of college living:

- Buy a lot of spaghetti and rice because it is cheap and not loaded with sodium. I lived on spaghetti and stir-fry throughout my late college career; and it helped me get fit. Buy whole wheat when possible, as it is more filling.

- Stay away from the frozen food aisles unless it is for vegetables because whatever you get will probably not fill you up, it will be loaded with sodium, and will probably be expensive and not worth the cost.

- Buy a lot of bananas because they are cheap and will get the job done just as well as an apple that costs three times as much.

- I highly recommend deli lunch meat over the packaged kind or constantly going out to eat, because it will save you money and time eating in.

- If you do go out to eat, research online for the specials at various restaurants so you can get a cheap meal that is not fast food.

- Try going without candy or ice cream, because for obvious reasons it is better for you; but also these products are expensive and if you don't have them for a month or longer you will no longer miss them or even really think about them.

- Try to make as much homemade cooking as you can because it is a great way to save money, you know what is going into your food, you can make as large of portions as you want contrary to buying prepared food, and girls are impressed when you can cook well. It will probably save you some bank later on when you offer to cook for a girl rather than take her out. It makes it look like you want some quiet alone time with her, when all you really want to do is save $25 from those bastards over at TGI Friday's.

- Have family dinner nights with friends where everyone brings something to the feast. It is a great chance to kick back and have a good well-rounded meal.

Summers Between School Years

Summers will be the most versatile part of your year because you have a great deal of options. You can stay and take summer classes, if you have an apartment stay in town and work, go home and work, go somewhere for an internship or travel around the country or the world. The options are endless for what you can do with the four months you have, rather than the three you had coming out of a year of high school. The extra time is rewarding to relax and tackle some things you were meaning to do during the school year.

The summer will also be about three weeks longer than it was in high school, to get back comfortable at home or in your apartment. But if you have nothing to do you will slowly lose your mind because you'll miss your college friends. You need to start deciding what you'll do for the summer in about January or February. Whatever it is, it should help your resume by adding relevant experience that goes hand-in-hand with your major and/or get you a lot of money to help pay bills or tuition. You don't want to be stuck just sitting around for nearly four months while others get an edge on you.

My first summer after my freshman year I had a sleep deprivation problem following getting very little sleep my spring semester of my first year. This was because of the way I scheduled classes, having early classes and they were spaced out just enough to allow me time to go back to my place but not enough to take a nap. The weather was also terrible most of the semester and I got a cold or mono that hung on for about a month and a half. By the time I came to, it was too late to find any employment; in fact I got rejected from K-Mart. That's right, K-Mart.

I grew up in a hometown of 450, where there are more cows than there are people. The summer following my freshman year was probably the most boring time of my life. I had spent a year away at school and able to play three hours of basketball a day and visit my friends in a short walk. Now I was relegated to mowing at my grandma's and having to drive 10-12 miles to visit any friends from high school. This was the summer I developed my newfound love for reading. I didn't even apply for internships or jobs; looking back in retrospect, I probably should have taken summer classes at Penn State-Altoona. Since I had the option to graduate in three and a half years without taking a single summer class, this would have opened up more options.

My area does not offer up much in the form of media outlets or working in sports (my chosen career path) as internships. It is a blue-collar town and the closest thing you will get to working in sports is re-stocking the shotguns in the display case at K-Mart. This opportunity would hardly help my career as an aspiring sports journalist at that point. I instead spent a great deal of time sleeping and getting healthy again. Regaining weight and going on family trips were the focus of the summer; but despite the love for my parents, we were spending entirely too much time together. I am sure they felt the same.

If you can't find a job that makes a lot of money or find an internship that relates to your major in some way after your freshman year, I recommend staying to take classes. It is hard to sit around and do nothing after having put the pedal to the metal for 8 ½ months doing school work and socializing. Taking classes and keeping the momentum going is a good option. Besides, you'll have a couple weeks between spring semester and summer, then summer going into fall. Also, summer classes tend to be easier because it really shows initiative that you decided to come and learn when your friends are out having fun in the sun.

Following my sophomore year, I got a hook up from my dad working for the Pennsylvania Department of Transportation. My partner on the job also went to Penn State and we ended up being good friends after 3 ½ months working together. I got really good pay at around $11 an hour and drove 300 miles a day to various parts of northwestern Pennsylvania. Usually I would drive to Ohio to take a number two just because I felt that was where it belonged. My actual job was checking to see if signs were present and calculate how much paint would be needed to re-paint the surface of the road.

Yes, as a journalism major I realize that this job had nothing to do with my future career but I was making good bank. As I said earlier, if you can't get a job during the summer in your profession go and make as much money as possible. I lived off of the $4,200 I made for pretty much the entire next school year, but I still was on pretty good track to graduating in four years on the button so summer classes were not a pressing issue. I probably should have tried to get an internship somewhere that would have helped me out, even if it were locally. Now people are asking me for clips of stories I've published for journalism jobs and I can't produce them because I never had a writing internship.

Following my junior year, I traveled to Las Vegas because I was 21 and had a terrific time. I made a decent amount sports betting and playing blackjack to cover many of my meals. I also played summer league baseball the whole summer while working a part-time job at Beaver Stadium. I figured I was all right in my journalism degree because I was working as an on-air host of a sport talk radio show. But I wasn't smart enough to realize I needed more to crack into the industry after I graduated. Getting outside of school experience I found out was also very important. Internships, internships, internships.

This part-time job of giving tours at Beaver Stadium is really what turned me onto wanting to work in sports administration. The job was enjoyable enough, except when I had to take school groups through because kids were loud and a few were not smacked around enough as they acted out. It took every ounce of energy I had not to roundhouse them. That summer I started considering the idea of going to graduate school for my master's degree as well.

Still at this point I have no writing experiences outside of class and online blogs on The Sporting News. I continued working at Beaver Stadium throughout my senior year, and worked at the club level entrance and met many of the incoming football recruits through the same entrance. Then after the school year when I graduated I started working for a site known as Pro Player Video that specialized in editing game tape for potential professional basketball players. The majority of our clients were foreign league or NBDL that the normal basketball fan has never heard of. Only the real nerds who know information about college basketball like a geek knows information about Star Wars would hear of many of our clients.

That is when I went to graduate school at Southern Mississippi to get my sports management degree and really catches us up to where we are now. I got a lot of insight into the industry and a great deal of hands on experience. I finished my master's degree in the summer of

2009; the first time I've taken summer classes. These classes were on Southern Miss's dime though considering I was a graduate assistant. I lived in State College and continued to work with Pro Player Video, where I get to see a small company grow even though I made very little money.

I'm still trying to scratch and claw my way into the field of athletics, and my not playing sports at the college level has hurt the quest. This goes back to picking your major and how no kid really knows what they want at age 18 or 19. If I had known for sure what specifically I wanted to do in sports I would have had an internship or two more than what I have. But it is so difficult to know what you want to know at such a young age that you will spend much of your early 20's making up for what you were lacking as a teenager.

I would say my regrets of the summers are few, but getting an internship working in athletic facilities and maybe traveling a little bit more would be all that is left desired. Employers often look at experience before they look at your school or GPA. I had a terrific time living the three summers I did in State College without the high demand of academics where I could just enjoy beautiful weather, sit outside for a drink, see my friends, and sleep in. Although professionally it hurt me, I think socially it kept me from going insane and helped me blossom.

Moving to a new place to do graduate school or an internship stinks because you don't know where is good to live or know anyone in most cases. To reach your dreams you have to take a risk, and I probably did not take as many as I should have to be where I want to be. But people always second-guess themselves and wish they could do something else. Change is good because you have to roll with the punches that are dealt to you and overcome obstacles like going other places because your options at home aren't there. You will have new experiences you wouldn't have had if you stayed in your own little bubble.

When you spend most of the year bundled up in a winter coat it is nice to be able to finally do some things outdoors. Living in a larger place such as State College there was all kinds of summer events to go to. I enjoyed the mid-summer Arts Festival in State College that lasts from Wednesday until Sunday that brought back many of my friends for the weekend. It is the lone weekend when no one has homework to worry about and can just go crazy one time to break the boredom of the real world. I also enjoyed all the art I come across from vendors from all over the country coming into this very large event. There are a lot of talented people out there doing some amazing things.

But the Arts Festival was just one of the many events I got to take in. I do wish I did not spend as much time sitting around during the day and would have taken more trips. My jobs were flexible and I never had a need to take summer classes until I got to graduate school so I could finish while the school paid for it. I always wanted to go to San Diego to hang out on the beach and see the zoo, but I never got around to doing it yet. I never had a car while living in State College because of the ridiculous parking rates and the school is not in most convenient place as far as air or rail travel.

To review, your first option would be trying to find a job or internship in your field to help build your resume. Secondly, if you can't get that find a job that gets you the most amount of money possible. You can handle any job for 3 ½ months to build up a nice little roll of money, because you have a foreseeable end date. Lastly, if neither is an option, goes take summer classes Build your professional portfolio, but don't forget your friends.

Wingmen

Picking wingmen to accompany you into any social setting is potentially one of the greatest challenges you will face in college. It is just as important as getting internships, getting good grades, and all that other junk. This cast of about 2-3 characters will be what pulls you through many troubling nights, whether it is intercepting the girl who is being a real anchor or walking you home when you've had too much to drink. These guys will be your most valuable social assets along with pretty girls to hang out with that enhance your image. They're like your guardian angels when they stick to the plan.

For those of you who do not know, a wingman is a guy who comes out with you to simply cancel out one of the friends of the girl you're trying to get with. He also is like a golf caddy offering a second opinion on whether you're making a good decision to avoid the dreadful, "I don't want to talk about it" morning. He is your lifeblood and you must scratch his back in the same way he is scratching yours. Sometimes you have to take the hit for the team, by hanging out with the girl who is 20 pounds overweight with an odd love for *Hello Kitty*. You just have to grit your teeth and do what your buddy needs to seal the deal that night. Your day in the sun is sure to come in the bar.

Girls typically do not like to break out and fly solo nearly as much as guys are willing to when they are out at the club. You can't try to talk to a group of girls on your own; you need a couple of guys with you anyways to be a decent package group. You need to have the credibility of other friends with you so it looks like at least you have some people who can put up with you and there is a trustworthy connection for other girls to meet guys. But after this encounter, guys are trying to break off one-on-one with the girls because as stated we can work independently a bit better than girls do. It is the reason why guys don't have group meetings in the bathroom at a party.

The rule is regardless of the outcome for the guy who needs help; he does not get any mulligans. You can't be greedy; you have to be able to rotate position in the group because the same guy can't always be diving on the grenade for the team or he'll develop a bad reputation. He will get disgruntled and leave the group for good, which causes a ripple effect for the remaining members as they adjust to his absence. It isn't even about looks in the group as to who plays what role; it is a sharing is caring rule that every group of guys needs to stand by. When an opportunity arises for one of the members to capitalize you need to act upon it. If your buddy can start dating a good-looking girl the odds of her having good-looking friends is quite good. Take advantage of that like it is a 3-on-1 break in basketball.

I had an epiphany at age 17 at the Pittsburgh Zoo. I saw a single elephant hanging out with a group of giraffes. I thought this was odd, but then noticed a group of girls walking by. Three of the four were gorgeous, but there was the one girl who was nasty looking and a completely mean self-centered person who looks out for the group. She will say things like "Let's get out of here," "this guy is a jerk," "let's have a girl's night," "we're just here to dance," and other worthless mumbles that cock-block you. You can't allow this to happen, thus a wingman jumping on the grenade to save the others will need to happen.

As we've noted three giraffes and an elephant in the group. As lovable as elephants are especially since the Disney classic *Operation Dumbo Drop*, these girls are only there to make sure if she can't have fun then no one can. For us guys it isn't that hurtful to drop the dead weight guy who is holding up the group, but women have something called emotions. The elephant (which doesn't mean she is fat, just a drag) is distinguishable from the giraffes based on no guys wanting to hit on her and she is usually very moody about absolutely everything.

You may be asking yourself "Why would a group of girls have just one unattractive girl in it?" That is a good question, but from talking to a number of friends (both male and female) the general conscience is that it is usually a girl who was at one time good looking, and still believes she is. Also a point brought up is the other girls wanting to feel better about themselves knowing that they are not the least attractive girl in the group. It is like not being the slowest gazelle whenever a pack of lions attacks.

If your wingman jumps on the grenade for the good of the group and takes this girl aside to talk and show the least amount of interest in, the rest of the group owes him. Whether it's free beer, food, or simply paying him back later through having to draw straws and bite the bullet at a later date, this man is a real patriot. Not only will he have to deal with her that night, but also because he did show interest there will without a doubt be a Facebook friend request and possibly a series of random text messages asking him what he's up to. Avoiding give your number is key, but not always possible. Sometimes she takes your phone and puts her number in there and texts herself. I've seen it before, and it is awful.

It isn't easy to lose a clinger either; you will get voice mails and texts if you were dumb enough to give her your number, but Facebook is a virtual guarantee. She will go through her friends to find your buddy, then through his friends to find and add you to her friend requests. This is not uncommon, and is a little weird, but it happens all the time and her amazing re-con work will be kind of impressive. You know darn well you don't have the energy or the resources (or possibly brain cells) to put together a research assignment like that.

Simply not answering the texts and messages won't be enough to slow her down sometimes, because you may have been her only nibble in months. This isn't always the case; most girls get the idea that you're not interested but not always. Like a starved fish she won't let go of that hook until you reel her in. But you'll be sure if you see her again, especially if your buddies had success with her friends. So you'll need to make up an elaborate but believable excuse to get out of the situation. She might end up being a nice girl to just hang out with, but is not your particular type of bourbon as far as dating wise.

Can any old guy be a solid wingman? No, certainly not because you need to have good chemistry with your wingmen that you are going out with. You have to enjoy the same bars and clubs; have somewhat similar interests; they can't be an anchor of a human being boring the girl he is trying to take out of the equation; and lastly he has to at least be able to attract women. You can't have a wingman that bores girls by talking to them about computer programming and *Dragonball-Z*. These are just a couple of the mindless conversation topics I've heard men talking to girls about that send shivers down my spine. These topics detract girls, and a good wingman should be able to keep a girl entertained and out of the equation for as long as his buddy needs. The longer she is entertained, the longer she is out of your hair.

It may take you six months or a year to find a solid group of guys to go out with. This certainly should be a point of interest as soon as you step foot on campus. You can't have deserters or socially awkward guys in the group because that puts more pressure on the others. You will need to develop chemistry to know each other's style in girls. Desperation levels will vary from day-to-day and this dictates the roles you will take throughout the night. These little details can be the difference between success and failure, especially with other groups of guys circling the girls. Many of the guys also making the moves will be just like you, but other will be the dreaded tools ruining men's reputation as they continue to breathe. It may take many times going out to develop the desired level of chemistry that will produce consistent success.

Much like a sports team it takes a while working together to know exactly what one of your wingmen will do. It is tough to just pick up a wingman out of nowhere and be successful. During my junior year my two wingmen fell into relationships so I had to find new ones to replace them. Ever since then it has been a revolving door of guys coming and going to help the cause with one another. I have a lot of friends so it has been a work in progress, but it took about a year to find a solid group of guys. Losing your wingmen is like getting knocked off your horse, it's all about getting back on.

Losing one of your wingman will throw off the momentum of the whole group. Girlfriends are as good as enemy snipers waiting to pick guys off one-by-one as they get into range. But those who survive will tell stories of horror and terror that will make even the most experienced tomcat shiver. The reserve for replacing your buddy who is now in a relationship never live up to standards off the bat, and your crew becomes a revolving door until you find someone who clicks. You just have to tip your cap to a lost wingman.

Finding women is not that much different than playing poker. You have to keep folding until you get something promising dealt your way. It is just a game of survival until your next big break. When that perfect hand comes along, push your chips all in and take the game. It is all about playing it smart, because I have a lot of friends who go all in on even the slightest promise of a good hand. Be careful because your actions affect your wingmen.

Generally your wingman should be well rounded with decent looks, an interesting personality, smart, and be able to handle himself drinking and on the dance floor. This way he is a trustworthy guy to keep a girl occupied all night while you work your magic with Ms. Right or Ms. Right Now depending on your mood. But finding these well-rounded guys to join your crew is a difficult task because other guys will be vying for their services on any given night. This is why you need to be friends with a group of these guys to insure yourself success.

I have a lot of friends who can play a good secondary role but not a great deal who have the whole package to be successful. We all have our flaws, with my own probably being my 5'9" height and young looks not working in my favor unless it is 18 and under night at the club. I have a friend who is probably the best assist guy in any group setting you up to look good for girls. He has a very strong way with words and using them to his advantage in a social setting to help you look good. When he is tomcatting it, he is just as good as anyone I know. But if he is seeing someone he simply takes a secondary role, because he can't put it all on the line. At best, guys in relationships can only play a secondary role but most times they don't even play that to help you out.

A wingman cannot deviate from the game plan and let his fellow group crumble in his absence. Sometimes his loss brings an unwanted girl back into the equation, which pulls the rest of the girls away from the group to do something stupid like going to a frat. But the game plan must be talked about briefly amongst the group before going in to talk to the girls. Adjustments are made on the fly much like the west coast no-huddle offense that many college and pro football teams use. You have to be well versed and know your teammates and predict where they will be for the play to work. With wingmen this is a similar philosophy. Good luck out there!

Girls

It is an awful thing to say but girls are more valuable than money in college. Going to parties or clubs your value as a guy rises with the number of girls you have with you, more specifically the more attractive girls you have with you. It is an awful fact of college life, but it is because the majority of parties are thrown by guys because they honestly do not care about the state of their apartment or house nearly as much as girls. Believe me I have been in some houses that should have been condemned after the year of parties in them.

When a guy working at the door sees a group of guys he sees money going down the toilet and a mess left behind. When he sees a group of girls, he sees an investment in the future prospects of his night. Getting a good group of good-looking girls early in your college career is like having an Easy Pass on the highway socially. It is way too tough to roll up with you and 11 of your good guy friends and hope to get into any party, especially if it is a frat brodeo.

As a freshman it is important to get decent alcohol, be as mature as possible without looking like a stuck up douche and make great girl friends that enjoy the nightlife. You don't need the most good looking girls to have a successful early run in college, but at least girls that can clean up well and attract the attention of a few lonely guys who are willing to spring for a few cases or a keg. But it is important not to lose tabs on these girls, and in fact make more contacts while with the girls.

The problem is that girls are physically ahead of guys peaking; so they look good a couple years before guys do. Essentially, you have freshmen girls who have not gained the freshmen 15 because they still have a good metabolism and a decent diet from living at home. On the other hand, very few guys have filled out so the muscle does not develop as fast. This development issue teamed with the fact that freshmen guys usually do not have breasts and can't buy alcohol is a bad combination for matching up with more mature older college guys.

As a young gun you have to make due and try to salvage what great girls you can to hang out with. The tides will eventually turn where those older guys graduate and you start eating that cafeteria food like a horse and put on weight; hopefully you're also exercise or you'll be the random beer gut guy who will get made fun of at future high school class reunions. This is when you start scoping out the freshmen girls coming in and befriend them. But be cautious, you can only do this for a year or two so pick wisely who you want to hang out with. After a year or two you're just a dirty old man; yet there are guys I know who are 25 or 26 who still try to hit on freshmen like some sort of weirdo.

Types of Girls

There are four categories of girls you will find early in college. They are the smoking hot socialites, the ugly duckling theory, middle of the road, and lastly an anchor to your success. On a side note, there is a side group known as old high school girlfriends that seriously inhibit your social development because if the bad news arises that you will be at the same college, have fun trying to make up ground on your single guy friends who have the time to party. You will be too busy watching "The Notebook" and spending random dinners at Olive Garden, while your buddies collect numbers like baseball cards.

The first group is the smoking hot socialites. These are the girls who no matter the guy you ask they will find this girl attractive just because she probably has a pretty face and a great body. These girls however are the most dangerous, and to put it in financial investing terms it is like buying a stock while it is high. You can only hope to ride this pipe dream for as long as you can because eventually these girls will figure out they are too good for you and go to older guys who can buy them fancy liquor or they will think they are too good for you and do the same.

Finances will be short so buying these girls a drink will probably be a poor investment. They'll like something that is not on the specials menu and know it. The bartender will have to pull a book out from behind the bar and charge you $9 for doing so. You offering to buy her a drink is just an invitation for her to get whatever she wants. If you're lucky enough for her to talk to you throughout the course of the drink consumption feel lucky, you're in elite company. You will probably be left with a meaningless smile and five or ten less dollars.

These girls are usually a huge tease and are very rarely truly nice. Once in a blue moon you will meet a dashingly good-looking girl who doubles as being a sweetheart. I had one such case while I was a freshman at PSU-Altoona who fit the description. I worked on multiple projects with her during my first semester of college. Being from a 450 person town, in which half the residents live in trailers, I never came across any trailer park treasures to speak of. This girl was smoking hot, I felt like a #16 seed going against the #1 in the NCAA tournament. Needless to say, no #16 seed has ever been able to overcome playing a #1 in the history of the tournament, as I was also out of my league.

Next you have the ugly duckling or the trailer park treasure girl who probably grew up in a small town. This girl was probably awkward as an early teenager, possibly with acne or braces and did not receive a lot of attention. Miraculously she has not developed the high nose/treat me like a princess tendency that many great looking girls do. These truly are the girls to go for because they tend to be nice because they did not always get what they wanted and have not yet adjusted to being constantly pursued.

I have always tried to pursue the girls who fit the ugly duckling phase. I do not want to go back to your mom's house and look at pictures of you at age 12-14 when you were goofy looking and all legs. Listen, I know I am no great prize and really cannot attain the smokin' hot girls. Those girls are for guys who will sacrifice their masculinity and pride and become douche bags to chase her. The ugly duckling is a beautiful butterfly fresh out of the cocoon. It is your job to not treat her like a queen, and like a normal person, so she does not get a big head and realize her value. This is just for making other guys around you jealous instead because you have a gorgeous girl who is also incredibly nice.

The middle of the road girls are the ones who become increasingly good looking as you get drunk, but are easily forgettable while you are in a normal sober setting. They are typically are nice girls, but can also be bitter and a real bore (refer to: Wingmen jumping on grenades). They are the type of girls that you like to hang out with, but never really consider dating because you assume you can do better. They can be girly, but also be one of the guys and sometimes you treat them like that.

These girls are dangerous though depending on how well they take care of themselves. They can easily become beautiful if they have a decent base to work with such as a pretty face, but maybe a few too many pounds on. These girls that can easily make the transition from just all right to more than worth the time and can be a decent project to invest in, especially if you can spend time together working out (because like I said you're probably no prize either).

The middle of the road girl is usually on the fringe of being a good prospect but like I said needs those few little touch ups to become pretty. But they can just as easily swing to the bad side of the fence that puts them far from desirable like putting on 30 pounds or just generally not fun to hang out with. This is when the girl can easily become the elephant in the "elephant theory reflecting groups of girls" that I mentioned in the wingmen chapter. Of all the group of girls this group is probably the largest out of sheer numbers who are teetering on that fence between a prospect and a scrapped project.

The last group is the girls are an anchor to your success because they are rarely good looking or nice and probably do not have that many friends. They probably also hate college and date some random unlucky sap online for whom she sent a picture to that was not her. But if the picture was her it was probably before she let herself go, or is the most flattering picture in her collection. But the guy who has to meet women on the Internet has it coming, because it is far from the way to meet women. Sorry to tell you Chemistry.com and E-Harmony, but I will not be using your products because my life is not hopeless.

But "The Anchor" to your social life probably also brings people down around you due to her lack of fun. She also probably has no girls who are good looking that you can use her as a hookup for, maybe if lightning strikes she may have an ugly duckling friend for you to work on. But I will highly doubt this because even the ugly duckling enjoys going out on a Friday night while "The Anchor" holds down the fort. Pun intended.

If you can't get girls, there will always be always strip clubs. The problem with strip clubs is you're usually a sad individual if you have to turn this option anyways. These girls just make it less hidden that they are only interested in you for your money. It would be far more cost efficient and creepy if you simply did some self-improvement. Strip clubs maybe the most honest business there is.

If you go with a group of guys there is always varying degrees of comfort found within the group. The guy who is least likely to have success in a traditional bar or party setting most times is the most comfortable guy in the strip club. Conversely, the guy who is most likely to get girls in a normal setting is most uncomfortable. This is because the guys who are not used to having to dump tons of money to impress girls are not used to having to reach for the wallet so often.

Oh you have a girlfriend, I'll see you at your wedding

If you do decide to be in a relationship, do not lose touch of your wingmen or your buddies. You do not want to be that guy whose balls are in your girlfriend's purse, and when she says jump you ask how high. These guys annoy all previous people who knew them, and to a group of single guys can be considered a cancer to the group. They are simply dead weight because all they talk about is their girlfriend and the drama going on in the relationship. Guys really don't care about your relationship; our needs are far shallower. We'd rather just get messed up and hit on some cute girl at the bar than hear any more about how she makes you take your socks off in bed or what you'll buy for Valentine's Day.

I've had friends handle having a girlfriend various ways, sometimes dumping us completely to spend time with the girl. There are also times when a guy still can't break away from the social life he had before and can't commit to the relationship. But 90% of relationships I've seen are somewhere in between, but it is still frustrating to lose one of the guys in your group even if it is just for a night a week. One of my roommates used to be ridiculous before meeting his girlfriend.

We would go to parties as sophomores and he would get 17 or 18 shots deep during the night and would stumble home. It was a great time because we always kept each other out of trouble and watched each other's backs. He used to take his pants off at a party or walk into a random apartment of someone we barely knew and grabbed one of their drinks and walked out. The night wasn't complete without him returning with his jeans in his arm, wearing a pair of basketball shorts underneath and having a color ring around his mouth from whatever fruity drinks he had that night.

But when he first got his girlfriend it was an awkward transition for the rest of us because we started seeing him less and he became far more conservative. We were never sure if it was a self-restraint issue or if he was simply getting owned by the girlfriend. We had a hard time getting to know the girl he was dating as well because she was very shy and reserved, but we ended up approving once she started opening up to us. She turned out to be an amazing girl. It was frustrating to lose our friend as a wingman, because losing him took something away from our group and our ability to work a room.

Then one of my other roommates started dating a girl who I had known longer than him. We loved them both and liked them being together, but the same thing happened. We would lose my other roommate for a couple nights a week, so I had to go outside my apartment to find my main reliable guys to go out on the town with. Once one of your friends gets a girlfriend they are dead to you, for all intensive purposes, when you go tomcatting at the bar with the guys.

Living and Learning

As far as myself I have always been single, literally my entire life. I'm an incredibly picky guy who thinks way too much about every situation, but not to the point of being awkward. I have definitely come a long way from my freshmen year where I was super shy around new girls. It was like throwing a little kid into a toy store; he wants everything and can't decide. I came from a high school of 80, so I knew all the girls in my grade since we were little kids. Adjustments had to be made when I got to college.

I used to be a guy who was really into girls that were blonde hair and blue eyes, which I've always referred to as California blondes. For some reason, this is what I dug throughout my early days in college but that eventually wore off. Now I don't really care, I like the girl when I see her, which I think is a good way to live. If you are too picky then you could miss out on someone great who may like you, but because of your particulars doesn't fit to your standards. I wish I had dropped my stereotypical standards earlier in college.

To be fair, I will discuss my success and failures to show I have some knowledge and credibility without the attachment of a relationship. I would say on average I would get between 7-10 numbers a month from various girls I met at bars, clubs, or class that were interested in hanging out. This is a little tough to hang out with all of these girls, and sometimes you're just being nice and taking the number with no real intention of contacting them. I would say I only keep or contact 50% of the girls. Sometimes I get to the end of the month and take a look at the numbers I've accumulated and have no idea who some of the girls are and delete them.

"Rupe, it's about quantity, not quality because if I talk to 50 girls in a night and 49 turn me down I still succeed." - **My friend drunkenly leaning on the bar (Circa 2006).**

This particular friend uses the Babe Ruth theory in that he is willing strike out 10 times in order to hit one home run. Not a bad approach, all or nothing; girls love that kind of confidence. It is a gutsy move talking to this many girls because you will have some repeats, and you essentially turn the game into checkers. I prefer to play a game of chess where you look for weaknesses in the girl's defense and exploit them. Despite this advice from a close friend I am quite particular in the type of girls I enjoy talking to; so his style is not my particular type of brandy.

In fact, I've only been truly interested in three girls throughout my college career that also had feelings for me: one as a sophomore, one as a junior, and one as a senior. Like an idiot I let the opportunities pass me by because I kept weighing the options between being in a relationship and being single in one of the country's top party schools. Is it really worth sacrificing where I night will go for the girl?

You live and learn. This is precisely why I am discussing my credibility and relaying the information I have learned to my readers. Two of the three girls I really liked instantaneously but did not think I really had a chance from the get go. But I wore on them probably from my sheer ridiculousness and random thoughts I have that can get even the sternest girl to laugh. I probably wouldn't have approached these girls earlier in my college career. The other girl ended up wearing on me after a lot of late night conversation, but once again the possibility of being single in a crazy atmosphere such as Penn State was too much.

In the case of the first girl, who I met as a sophomore she was kind of bubbly and always upbeat. We hung out a lot late at night, but had a great deal of different views on subjects, which does not necessarily bother me. I like a girl who is not afraid to speak her mind and tell me what she thinks and wants because it makes my job easier and allows me know she is intelligent. This was the case of this girl who often did a great job of keeping me in line and would not back down.

The second girl I met early in my junior year and was probably more like me than any other girl I met in college. In fact, I always felt like she was a half step ahead of me thinking almost all the time and nothing I did had any shock factor. She was very laid back, but not afraid to be a little crazy at times to keep it interesting. We had a great deal of pressure on us from surrounding friends to be together, which was really annoying. I have to thank my friends for being supportive, but sometimes it is too much to let things come together naturally. I liked her a lot from the first time I met her, but she was shy and I had no idea she liked me as well until long after the opportunity was over.

We would only hang out every couple weeks, which made it really difficult for me to make any headway in the situation. I wasn't as mature as I probably should have been and should have tried to make a better effort than I did. I kept living my life in my apartment that always had the beer pong table up and a fridge full of beer to go along with it. When I found out she also liked me at the same time it was a crushing blow, but shows you that you need to act on how you feel.

The last girl and I really never had a chance. I knew her from earlier in my college career, but she had a boyfriend at the time. She didn't admit that she liked me until right before I left for Mississippi, which would have made it a tough venture. What made it even tougher was that she and I went to separate campuses for our last two years of college. She's a great girl to this day and plays off of her emotions all the time, which is something I admire. In this case, it was just bad timing, which is a part of life.

Meeting Girls and Tips for Success

Your first year you want to get your tight group of friends with a nice mix of a handful of guys to hang out with and be associated with, a solid group of girl friends who can hook you up with their connections, and get yourself on the right academic pace.   I did all right getting numbers from girls my freshmen year, but I really needed to develop some game. It didn't help that I looked like I was 14 years old as a college freshmen. But I had to rely on my humor and intelligence because of my really young looks had girls making assumptions about my maturity.

When you are a freshman, you spend a lot of time using friends who have older family members or friends in college and may have an apartment and hookup to alcohol. The other option is going to fraternities; I spent my time going to their parties despite my distaste for the fraternity guys who often weren't the best to the girls that were with me. Knowing that my young look was not to my advantage, it became quite apparent I would have to turn to my intelligence and charm.

Some guys I know are intelligent but horrible with girls because that talk to girls about the things they know most about such as computers, taxes, finance, and other non-attractive subjects. Even talking about your incredible knowledge of sports is most likely to put you in the friends-zone or worse yet, not even on the radar. An approach I used was making absolutely every meeting look like a coincidence to talk to the girl.

For instance, if I saw a girl was going through the salad bar in the cafeteria I would go stand looking at the fruit next to it. I would just stand there pretending as if I cared about the decision between a banana and an apple until she slowly worked her way down to me. It usually led to a few minute long conversations about fruit and weather, but it at least broke the ice. Later, if I saw the girl I would have a reference point to go back to, and she was usually amazed that I remembered the meeting.

Furthermore, I always made a point of memorizing a girl's name and where she was from because once again if I saw her again she would be amazed that I remembered such facts. These little things seem pointless but for whatever reason girls care about it. Don't ask me to break down the human brain and point to the part of the brain that cares about this because I almost always fail science courses. You would probably have better luck with an 11-year old in middle school when it comes to biology or anatomy.

Another example of using intelligence is making sure you and a buddy get to the first class of the semester 10 minutes early and scope out one of the best looking girls there. Act a little frustrated about being in the class and strike up an immediate conversation with your friend about the class, tossing in some humor here and there. Eventually if you're not an idiot about it, the girl will laugh and then she'll be forced to turn around and join in the conversation. You'll strike up a conversation, most likely will do a project together and develop a line of contact. You're setting the table for the future and that's not just academics, but social.

Girls Love Gay Dudes

Every now and then you will run into the girl who calls and texts you to meet her and her friends out that night at the bar. You get a hold of your wingmen to meet up with the girl that night and you have certain friends of hers in mind who she usually hangs out with. You spend the evening talking up the girls she hangs out with and how your boys have a chance. Once you finally get your buddies convinced to come out to the bar you pre-game with a few drinks to have a buzz when you walk into the bar.

You get to the bar and order a drink and look for your friend who is talking to two or three other dudes. Then you start to wander over to her and say hello to a few friends on your way over with your guys. But when you ask her who her friends are, she introduces you to her gay friends, with whom she told you were excited to meet. The meeting is awkward both for the gay friends and your wingmen, but most of all yourself. The girl gets out scathe-free and blames it on a lack of communication. You kindly talk to the group for an hour or so and then scope out some girls that you want to talk to.

Don't get me wrong; it has been enlightening to get to know many gay people. It is a different perspective on the world and they seem to pick up on girls' subtle hints better than you do. Sometimes if you're lucky they relay this information onto you kind of like a pitching coach in baseball talking through strategy.

Call the Bomb Squad She Has Glitter

Glitter is something that is used periodically by girls to gain more attention to them (I'm guessing). But one speckle of this junk on your shirt will make you look like a pixie, and your buddies won't let you forget it. That is until it happens to them. Whoever the horse's ass was that invented this is very rich somewhere making every man's life miserable.

My hatred of glitter goes back to a Valentine's Day card my roommate received. He saw something on the bottom of the package, but didn't know what it was so he carelessly opened the package. Next thing we know, we have a full-scale glittery mess on our hands all on our kitchen floor and counter. It was a lost cause as the glitter stayed on the floor until the day we moved out. Nothing short of a black hole can suck this stuff up from carpet or floors. Be careful and strongly discourage glitter of any kind, even years later when your kid comes home with an art project. Tell them to take it right to the trashcan, because there is no way that is coming in our double-wide palace.

Dating

When you finally go on a date with one of these girls that you've scoped out to talk to and probably researched, or followed on Facebook, there are certain ground rules that must be done. You need to take her to a non-threatening environment like a decent mid-range restaurant for dinner (lunch sends out a friends vibe), so you don't have to spend a ton of money on the first date but you don't look like a cheap bastard making her order from the dollar menu. If you take her to a fancy restaurant you may come off as desperate and way over the top for something serious when all she is looking to do is find out more about you.

I'm personally a fan of cooking for a girl and having her get involved with cooking with me. It lets you do something together, and you communicate, save some money, and have some fun. If the meal isn't very good, then you're not out much money and it is both of your faults. It makes it look like you care enough about her to put out the effort to learn something new to try to impress her. That and I don't know a single girl who doesn't like a guy cooking for her.

The important thing to understand is putting out a good first impression on the first date. The rule is whoever asks the other person to go on the date pays for it, but as guys we know this is not the reality. You will end up having to pick up the check, or 50/50 at best on the first date. I find that it is necessary to wear a polo shirt or a button up on a date because it is a safe bet to not over or under dress for the girl on this date. Much like the restaurant, you want to come out strong but not over the top. But you do not want to look like a slob either.

After you've finished the meal and leave the standard 20% tip (because it makes you look generous), it is nice to think about the route that is necessary to get to either walking her back to her place or to a car. If the date went crappy take the direct route, if it went well go the roundabout way. This way you can find out more about her. I don't want to end up like my freshman college math teacher at Penn State-Altoona who used to make math equations to illustrate how his wife spent all his money.

On a side note, you could pull a dirty trick I learned from my high school friend's dad. He would go on dates with girls to somewhere nice and only order something small knowing the girl would never order a larger meal. This would save him money until he dropped the girl off, and he would swing by McDonald's on his way home. To approach was to save money and put out the impression that he is a guy who is willing to take a girl out to a nice dinner. It is sneaky, but oddly appealing for a guy on a limited budget.

The Levels of Maintenance

Here is some food for thought; do not call a girl high maintenance. I once made this mistake one night after my junior year to a girl who was spending all night complaining about her problems. I hadn't seen the girl in a few months and I knew she was rather dramatic a lot of the time, but still a pretty great girl to hang out with. Her friends were getting fed up with all the complaining and moaning all night and decided to walk way out in front of us, which she whined about.

Eventually we got to the intersection where my apartment was and I told her I was going home instead of going to the party. I would rather drink a beer and watch late-night Cinemax than listen to this trail of tears any longer. I told her she was "high maintenance" for which she yelled at me for calling her that. But I do not think she understood the meaning behind what I meant. So I never ever saw her again, but it was a sacrifice that needed to be made for the good of her life.

There are three types of girl personalities that guys have to deal with and they all have their ups and downs. You have high maintenance girls who tend to be the ones who spill their guts out when drunk and constantly want drama. Their emotional highs and lows will make you want to crash your car into an embankment just to not hear anything more about the dirty look she thought she got from the guy who you keep telling her had a glass eye. But she will probably be very particular and have a nice clean place and will look good, I mean really good. But they are usually the girls who you will have to wait all night for to get ready like I warn about. These girls take the patience of a saint to deal with.

Then you have normal girls who are straight down the road who really aren't too dramatic unless it really hits the fan. These girls will be cleaner than you and generally nice girls; but they will still keep you in line. I would say about 75% of girls fit into this section on the maintenance scale because they see low and high maintenance girls and don't want anything more to do with them than you do. These girls will probably be the one you will most likely want to settle on because they're fun and you won't want to drink yourself insane.

Then you have low maintenance girls who are fun to hang out with, but they seem more like a guy. Ugly duckling syndrome girls tend to fit in this category for a while until they realize they are pretty and somehow sneak out of your league. But for the most part these girls do not care what they look like and were probably raised like boys, which really is not their fault. They will probably be girls you can talk to sports and camping with fairly easily, sometimes easier than some of your guy friends, which can be a little creepy.

Girls Love Taking Pictures Like They're Investigating a Crime Scene

Girls will want to take pictures, lots of pictures because they realize that their college days will not last forever and so they treat every night like it's the prom. They will need to get a photo with absolutely every person who is out with them, then a group photo where they flag down a stranger, then just the girls, just the boys, then just her with the boys, and the list is endless. By the end of the night you will go to sleep with little flashes still burned into your corneas. Northern girls like the teapot stance and southern girls like the hand on the guy's chest stance. It is a social phenomenon that can't be explained.

All these pictures won't happen at just one place; every place you go that night she will reset the process. As she meets up with people she knows there will be more pictures to be taken; so get ready to be poked on the shoulder 15 times that night to be asked if you mind taking a photo. You do mind after about two or three, but you do not have the guts to say so. This girl will undoubtedly come back with a stupid line about it taking more muscles to frown than it takes to smile.

This is when you curse the invention of the digital camera because of its ability to take 2,000 photos and even go back to delete them so there is room for more. You actually start craving the days when people used disposable cameras for these outings and half the pictures came out poorly. But don't worry by the time you wake up six hours after you passed out the previous night, this girl will have posted 110 photos with you in 16 of them. The saddest part is this girl has never worked in film nor does she plan to; but still is in over 3,000 photos which makes you wonder exactly how much of her life has been eaten up by posing for photos.

Proof Some Girls Love Being the Center of Attention Part 1

There are a large percentage of people who like to be the center of attention; guys who are simply douche bags, tools, or peacocks to garner the attention. Girls are different. As guys our minds are not nearly as complex, so we deal with less dramatic issues and our man needs are what we focus on. Girls know how to play on this, especially in the dance club. They will dance all dirty like they want someone to come up to them; then will look disgusted once someone does. This is highly confusing to men as a whole.

There are quite a few stupid songs you will hear in the club that girls will go nuts over regardless of their age, I'm only going to address a couple as examples. The song "Beautiful Girls" by Sean Kingston every girl thinks she is a star in which I suppose was the point of Mr. Kingston, but then us guys have to deal with that ego boost the rest of the night. Another land mine I run into is "Girls Just Want to Have Fun." When this nuclear missile goes off, get off the floor because no girl will want to dance with you. They will simply want to grab the hands of other girls and dance together with any girl to show everyone that they indeed want to have fun.

Just go to a karaoke night to find all the divas and American Idol wannabes. Now we don't mind the occasional guy who is hammered and doesn't know what he is doing, because he is hilarious singing Eddie Money. That drunk guy is the very reason why we even showed up to karaoke night at the bar. But the two girls who go up every third song make you want to make it an unplugged night at the bar pretty damn fast. By unplugged I mean no singing whatsoever.

Weddings: Proof Some Girls Love Being the Center of Attention Part 2

Subtle hints, girls get them, why can't we?

The idea of subtle hints is as baffling as Area 51 or the location of Jimmy Hoffa. We don't know that you want roses on Valentine's Day because that is what Samantha likes in Sex in the City. You mentioned this seven months ago, while I was out grilling and pretending I cared about what you were mumbling. But still you insist that you told us that roses were your favorite and these daisies are for cheap bastards. We're sleeping on the couch, game over.

Women like to turn a relationship into an episode of CSI: *Miami* complete with fingerprints, autopsies, and crime scene scans, and a lineup. Their emotional capacity is like a warehouse and ours is a tollbooth in comparison. Your little booth couldn't possibly handle the entire inventory that she has going on in her crazy head. We just wish that subtle hints were more like *Blue's Clues* where you simply put a blue paw prints on three items and we put them together. For example, a paw print on Valentine's Day on our *Hooter's* calendar, a paw print on the Rose Bowl shirt we have, and one on some dandelions you picked out of the side yard across from *Kinko's*. See, this is much easier for everyone involved!

Treat Girls Well Because You'll Probably Be Cursed With a Hot Daughter

You are eying up great looking girls all day, and sometimes you go home and have to treat a sore neck. Days like "The First Day of Skirts" and every night out during 70+ degree weather are the leading causes of sore neck syndrome in college towns. But do we ever consider the fathers in this, when we're taking a good gander at Jennifer as she passes in the spaghetti strap white tank top and short gym shorts? No, we don't ever consider poor dad who is trying to defend his daughter like King Leonidas defending Sparta.

One day the tides will turn as you and Jennifer make a wonderful baby girl. She will grow up and you will be very close teaching her softball and how to drive. Then boys will start coming over because they are taking interest in your daughter who you still see as a little girl. That's when you glare at the guys she is bringing in who will probably have a "tool-like personality" and you will realize it: "God no, I have a hot daughter." Pretty soon you're going to K-Mart buying guns and ammo magazines, which will be placed right inside the front door of the house.

Your wife and daughter won't understand your new obsession with killing and being incredibly manly. They may even find you barbaric and psycho for throwing out your model car collection and instead replacing it with a gun rack next to your mounted deer head you bought at a flea market. They will scratch their heads when you have a bench and weight set on the front porch. They don't really understand, but that is when you realize life has come full circle, and now you're on the defense. Now tool shed Johnny will be eying up your little girl while she's at college, while you take mixed martial arts classes to protect her at all costs.

Reasons Why Girlfriends Make You Add 10 Pounds of Beer Weight

When a guy gets his girlfriend, there are certain goals set out by the friends of the guy who takes the plunge. Initially, you try to find common ground with the girlfriend for your buddy's time, but you never make an issue out of it. You don't want to upset her or your friend who has decided to make this commitment, but there is some negotiating going on behind his back. Now he has to share his time and do mutual couple things and potentially make some changes in his life, for the better as she sees it. Guys are not lost puppies that need groomed and their friends are not a bunch of nomad hobos who are a bad influence. A relationship takes time and patience of all the parties involved. But make no doubt about it; we are at war.

Occasionally, as a guy entering a relationship there will be things that you need to sacrifice. Most notably your beer bong, taste in movies, and collection of bobble heads you've collected from giveaways. She will dominate the relationship, and there isn't much we can do about it, so time management skills are needed. I can't think of a single friend that hasn't changed in a major way after being in a relationship for a long time. It is like that 1,000 yard stare you hear about in war movies.

Some girls take forever to get ready. It is always a good idea to tell her a party starts 20 minutes earlier than it does so that you will only be a half an hour late. If the girl comes out anything less than looking her best after 75 minutes, or roughly the length of a Disney movie (credits included), there will be hell to pay. It is often smart to buy a six-pack on the way over, or simply bring a flask so you can keep the buzz going that you started 90 minutes earlier with your buddies. If worse comes to worst you can leave the beer in her fridge, which is a lot safer than taking it with you because some ass will always snag a beer from your six-pack and think you (A.) won't care or (B.) won't notice. They couldn't be more wrong.

The key is to not get mad at her, unless it is an absolute necessity to be where you need to be. An example is your own birthday party or a sporting event you're paying to see. You couldn't give a damn about an opera that she wanted to go see and being late; actually you would rather just sit in her living room watching re-runs of Fresh Prince of Bel-Air than go to that. You are willing to flush the $80 down the drain, and allow her to take the blame for being late to miss that earache festival.

But if she is making you late for tip-off of a basketball game or kickoff of a football game, you need to get on her like it is the last chopper out of Saigon. This is definitely a time to make an honest mistake telling her that the game is starting 30 minutes earlier than it actually does, because you know it will take her 15 minutes to put stupid paw prints under her eyes and ask your opinion on whether you like how she looks. You couldn't care less if she wore a raincoat and a straw hat; you want to get there for tip-off.

Another pressing issue is the cell phone because it contains the numbers of other girls, texts, voicemails, and calls. Do not let your girl get your cell phone and search through it; conversely, do not be the least bit curious about her phone and who is contacting her. If you are that insecure about your significant other than you probably shouldn't be in the relationship to begin with. I have never been through a girl's cell phone because you might stumble onto something you don't care to find out about one of her friends. However, don't give out too much information, because if you break up she will remember that garbage and could possibly be a town squire of your business to whoever will listen.

I have seen countless fights involving cell phones over the years because of someone searching through the other's phone. Does she pay the bill on your phone? No? Well, then she has no business going through it. If she does go through your phone, she is a psycho and you should probably gradually back out of the relationship, because psychos kill people. The only reason she should ever use your phone is if hers is dead (and there is no pay phone around) or you're on the ground dying and 911 needs to be called, but you crushed her phone on your fall to the ground. I would suggest a tight string and a tin can before I would give her my phone, because letting her see your phone means she is allowed to read your texts.

It is important to monitor the amount of alcohol that your girl takes in as well. Men are pretty simple when it comes to getting torn up; we just become more aggressive whether it's with girls or punching some random object. But then we eat a couple slices of pizza downed with a bottle of water and fall asleep. But if your girl gets drunk you are responsible for her and you won't know what to expect the first time she is in a train wreck wasted state. You may have the girl who is surprisingly cool; you could have suppressed urges to be a slut, the baggage check, or the wanderer. You always pray for the under control drunk girl who isn't horrible to deal with when you need to babysit her at a social event. I would say this is probably 75-80% of girls who are able to drink without the emotions coming out. But occasionally you get one of the other demons to come out, and you find out why that girl who is a 9 out 10 on the great looking scale was on the market.

The first demon is the girl who instantaneously becomes a huge flirt to every guy she talks to except you. She is naturally curious about other men deep down, and alcohol makes her act on the feelings she usually suppresses. She will go dance with other guys and it will test your patience as long as it doesn't cross the line to the guy trying to take her home. Babysitting this girl and trying to get her to stop drinking will become one of your priorities every night you go out as a couple.

The next beast to slay is the baggage check girl who gets emotional every time she gets wasted. She will cry and throw hissy fits when something isn't going her way during the night. She may get in a fight or two in the club while she has been drinking, which makes you awkwardly jump in between to break it up. You may even take a punch to the face or a claw mark from someone's nails to the face. Cat fights are terrific to watch, but not when they involve your girlfriend or end up on your lap.

Be prepared to stay up until 4 AM to get this girl to calm down and talked through her emotions. The weird part will be she will wake up well rested the next day and not recall anything that happened. You, on the other hand, will be absolutely wrecked and develop more questions than answers by your girl's drunken rave. Make a note these girls will probably be throwing up like a snow blower all through the night, crying, and yelling at you to get the Ritz Crackers in the kitchen that don't exist.

Every once in a blue moon, you come across the wanderer drunk who will leave you scratching your head at the end of the night. One moment you're having a great conversation, and you tell her you will be back in a minute to either go buy drinks or visit the gentlemen's facility; but when you get back she is gone. She just had an urge for pizza or a hamburger and got up and left without telling you where she went. You try to call but all you get is "I'm going down the street," "I'm just so hungry," or better yet her giving you a play-by-play of her walk, or shall I say stumble, to her next random location.

Odds are when she will forget what she wanted halfway to her destination then come up with a new place to go or see someone she knows. She may even see a dog to pet that distracts her. But when you finally wiggle the information out of her on where she was originally headed, she won't be there. Your night will turn into a real life version of Where's Waldo? Only your game is called "Have you seen my trashed girlfriend, because it's like tracking Osama Bin Laden?"

Another thing that will bother you is she will have the need to have girls' nights out. This is not the bad part because it is annoying to be with one person all day, every day, all year. The bad part is she gets to dictate when the day is, and she won't let you know until the day of. This is way too late for you and your buddies to pick up a case of beer to pre-game for a night at the Go Karts or a Medieval Times outing. At best you will be able to put together a small group of guys and hit up a local bar while your girl is out having the time of her life for an event she has been planning for a month.

From an outsider's perspective, girls' night outs are dangerous. It is a trap for guys because the group of girls just looks like too easy of a target. It is like a bar mirage. It is usually a group of 4-7 girls just dancing together in the middle of the floor, dressed kind of scandalously, and looking like they want attention. Many men fall into this trap of trying to dance with one of the members, only to have another girl in the group pull the girl back and look at him disgusted. This will continue the entire night until the girls all get hammered drunk on Washington Apples and Red Headed Slut shots causing them to split up because their needs get the best of them or they leave. Pray for the former as a single guy; but if your girlfriend is in this group pray for the latter.

Guys do not have guys' night outs where they don't want to talk to women. This is an inconceivable thought for men, because even when you're in a relationship you draw back to your instincts of checking out girls and challenging yourself. Competition is in our blood.

Yet another thing that will bother you is that some girls will want you to dress more "mature" in her eyes, but a cupcake in your mind. This will be give and take because some parts of your wardrobe you will take pride in, while others can go. Do not let her turn you into one of the members of "The Guys You Will Probably Hate" list I have assembled in a chapter coming up, it is walking a delicate line before falling into one of these categories. Do not let her take you away from the nice polo, a ball cap, and boot cut jeans into wearing a sports coat, over-sized sunglasses and some type of odd slip-on leather shoe just so you can be her little puppet. Keep your own style!

Better yet you get to keep your style, and in case you break up you won't have to take a trip to Goodwill to dump off that clown costume she made you wear. But at least listen to what she tells you when you guys go shopping for future reference and consideration to improving yourself.

She will probably want you to come over and watch television shows that you have no interest in. My one roommate made an easy transition because he has the television taste of a 25-year-old woman anyways; but rarely will this be the case jumping into a relationship. She will try to change it to some VH1 or E special show about some sort of pop culture icon that is being hounded by the paparazzi; something you probably don't give a damn about. But you have to think, that when we watch ESPN it is kind of the same thing that we are going through watching that garbage television that we are putting them through. But at least ESPN doesn't have Flavor Flav or Rock of Love.

To avoid watching stupid television, you realistically would rather watch paint dry than tune into suggest renting movies. It makes you sound like you want a quiet romantic evening, when all you really want to do is avoid watching two hours of Will & Grace on Lifetime. Turn it into a game where she picks out something she thinks you both would like, while you just go pick out what you want to watch. Rent the movies without seeing what the other picked out until they are already on the register; then she is trapped. Don't even take her into consideration when picking out your movie, because it could back fire into you watching The Notebook and Sweet Home Alabama in the same night.

To extend on this movie note, girls will often wonder why love is not like what she sees in the movies. She doesn't seem to understand that movies are made for entertainment, and the more extraordinary coincidences and craziness, the better the sales will be. Love is not actually like it is in the movies, because the majority of things that men do in those movies would be deemed socially crazy by others. Real love doesn't have a team of 15-20 writers and a $50 million budget to work off of, and your girl needs to realize this.

Women have all had their reference movies to point to as annoyance to men; your grandma points at Gone With the Wind, your mother has An Officer and a Gentlemen and Pretty Woman in the Richard Gere thanks for nothing era, and your girlfriend has The Notebook for you to live up to. Well saddle up for life sweetheart, because this is as good as it's going to get. Don't ever say that to her, but certainly don't try to replicate those movies. Nothing short of an act of God and Powerball victory will make her dreams come true.

Sometimes girls will try to blame certain events as being around that time of the month. I fear that five-day section of the month with my life. Most girls are OK, but some girls I have noticed you just have to get out of dodge. It is hard to tell what your girl will be like during that time of the month, especially because she will have no more need to impress you and can be her true self. I really hope you don't end up with the grizzly bear that wants to slice and dice you for picking up the wrong kind of cheese for her burger.

Girls will often say that guys have a time of the month as well. I agree with this, but it usually correlates with the loss of a favorite team or the time when all the bills hit at once after blowing $300 in Vegas. I throw stuff around after one of my favorite teams loses a game they shouldn't. It is a heat of the moment thing though.

Lastly, a deadly deed that girls do is the awkward bro-blind date where she continually tells you that you will love this guy that she knows.

This is somewhat caring that she knows someone she thinks you would be a good friend with. On the other hand, she may be trying to replace your best friends with a pre-approved selection of hers who is into fine wines. She will go on and on about this random guy that she knows and keep talking him up until you get to whatever social function you're supposed to meet him at. When you finally get there, you won't know anyone and your girlfriend will introduce you to this guy.

Your girl will then proceed to leave you alone with this guy in the kitchen where you will make small talk about the weather and sports for a while. It will be awkward, really awkward for both parties. Not quite like dropping a plate of spaghetti in the high school cafeteria awkward, but awkward enough. If you are lucky he will feel just as weird about the situation, which speeds up the drinking process to fill silences and could lead to a drunken conversation. Ideally, this guy will not be with his other guy friends, because you will be quickly dumped and relegated to the couch drinking your beer by yourself as the cliques of the party go together. If you're lucky a weird kid will come over and talk your ear off or someone will set off a fire alarm.

You will never say anything to your girlfriend about the odd situation she put you in, but you pray she never does it again. You do not appreciate being sent on bro-dates when she is just going to hang out with her friends; you'd rather sit at home and put together a jigsaw puzzle of a picture of Kentucky bluegrass yard than ever have to go through that again. Needless to say if you make it through the night, your girl owes you a little something that you will be able to bring up at a later date.

At some point you will have to go home and meet the parents, but the girl always gives you a forecast for the trip, which will be inaccurate. You never really know what to expect; you could get the easy-going father or you could get the guy who shows you his gun collection when you walk in the door. It is important to be impressive on these trips, not only to get approval, but also to become buddies with the dad. He is the only one who may have the true scouting report to the Rubik's cube that is your girlfriend's head. In fact, this guy may be cooler than your girlfriend. You may come over to just hang out with her Dad more than your girlfriend. This guy may like firecrackers and skeet shooting too.

I highly suggest not being a tool shed while you're at her house. No father wants you jumping in to help with icing cookies with his wife. He knows that his daughter has plenty of girlfriends; she doesn't need another one. What she needs is a man. Just be yourself, except for the parts about subscribing to "Barely Legal" and playing flip cup on a "Slow Down: My Daddy Works Here" highway signs. Her dad wants someone to hang out with, but also is tough enough to take care of his little girl. He doesn't want a pansy, but he also doesn't want a Charles Manson hard ass on his hands.

Appropriate Attire at Social Events

To assist with this chapter I brought in two girls who not only have a great fashion sense, but also gives a new perspective to the brands and articles of clothing you choose to wear. Brittany and Christen are two of my closest girl friends and often give me a lot of input about fashion. I trust their judgment because of their high intelligence and the fact they often out class me.

"Clothes, while very important, are NOT the first things we look at. Physical appearance and personality are far more important, even at a first glance. Clothes can be changed, fixed etc. What you see a guy wearing on a given night can give you one impression, but it may be completely different the next day." - Brittany and Christen

To justify myself I will say with confidence that I was a work in progress when it came to style going into college. I was a cargo pants, white basketball shoes, t-shirt, hooded sweatshirt, and a dirty hat wearing type of guy. This wasn't unusual coming from an area where you spent much of your time outdoors in the woods getting dirty. But you need to dress for success in college, academically and socially, to look as if you will be successful and are professional. This doesn't mean being like every other freshmen on the first day of class who stick out like a sore thumb putting in 45 minutes worth pre-class preparation for how they look.

Freshmen are the only people dressed up outside of employees on the first day of class; upperclassmen have been through at least a year of classes and realize there is no dress code. People will care less and less as each day passes and laundry piles up in the corner of apartments and dorm rooms. I was no exception, and often pushed articles of clothing to the limit because it was my natural mentally to wear clothes out before buying new ones. Showing up to class in a Trans-Am shirt and a dirty Braves hat was socially acceptable to me.

I don't suggest dressing up like it's the prom for the first day of classes, but I do suggest going with a little more style than I did. Freshmen don't realize they will grow tired and they will start slipping up by showing to class with a 5 o'clock shadow and sweat pants as soon as the weather gets crappy. Since I have a perpetual 5 o'clock shadow, this was just a staple of my livelihood. But getting laundry done at least every other week will be key into keeping up appearances as being serious about class and attracting girls. Simply, no girl wants any guy who smells like gasoline and body odor sitting next to her. I know this because I had a girl shoot me down because I smelled like gasoline after helping out a friend whose car ran out of fuel and I walked the fuel from the gas station and dumped it into her tank.

You see, upperclassmen have been through jobs and internships that the freshmen have not and realize the real world makes you wear nice clothes to the job. College is one of the last times you can dress like a bum and it is still acceptable, because no one really gives a damn what you're wearing just that you're there paying tuition. A college student does not have a consistent schedule so you might as well be comfortable in a nice t-shirt and a pair of basketball shorts. You will probably be in and out of your place all day, so it is dumb to change clothes every time you leave. You also have to squeeze in your time at the gym and if you have your shorts on under some sweatpants that's even better for you.

You invariably have one guy in every class who takes the not giving a damn about how he looks to the extreme. This could mean long shaggy hair, unkempt patchy facial hair, a lack of shower, wrinkled and/ or dirty clothing, and so much more. He will push the envelope so far as to no one really wanting to do a project with him and girls don't want to talk to him. Regardless of what time the class is or how the weather is outside this guy always looked like he just woke up and smoked a bowl. You certainly don't want to be this guy, but you don't need to dress like you're going out on a date either.

There are certain times of the year that are terrific for dressing up. There will be all kinds of parties like CEO/Corporate Hoes parties, Toga parties, 90's retro parties, favorite famous couple, and a bunch of other wacky ideas. Also job fairs will be a great time to dress up and also fall victim to all the girls dolled up to flirt with potential employers for internships. As a guy you will have to get used to good-looking girls getting everything in college from internships, to easy promotional jobs, and free drinks. It's just the way life is, and it sucks but you can deal with it.

On a side note, you will learn to love Halloween not because of what you wear, but for the girls. Girls have roughly eight billion outfits for Halloween, but all of them are somehow crossbred with a prostitute outfit. There is absolutely nothing wrong with this, because I could easily just take a six pack and sit on the corner with a lawn chair and watch girls go by and have just as good of time as I would going to a party. I enjoy the classics: sexy witch, sexy cop, sexy fire fighter, nurse, or just a flat out general prostitute.

Another thing to note about Halloween is the size of your costume. Without a doubt someone will show up as the Solar System, a horse or something huge and stupid that will take up a bunch of room. Party space is at a premium in small college apartments, so don't be a jackass and wear something huge like dressing up as a school bus. Try to be as creative yet take up the least amount of room as possible, I usually just buy some garbage from Wal-Mart's clearance rack and make a costume out of whatever I find. Most years I wore a normal outfit and an eye patch. No one seemed to mind.

At college it'll be the first time you will be amazed at the sheer number of clothes that every girl has. As guys, we just have one selection of clothing that runs us the whole year because most of us absolutely despise shopping. But girls have a winter and a summer collection of clothes. I've even met a few girls that have a spring/fall collection, which they rotate throughout the year. Their collection of clothes for each season is the size of your collection of crappy t-shirt, dirty jeans, and sweatshirts that you have assembled from Christmas and various activities you participated in. Girls will be wearing a $30 Abercrombie t-shirt while you'll be wearing a shirt that says "We Suck" that you got from blood bank along with a free sandwich.

This is when you first realize what girls are not worth dating because they could be an eventual drain on your bank account. Their dad just gives them the credit card or $200 and they hit the mall, not realizing the value of hard work and a dollar. This is the case for all or even many girls, but I have run into a lot of these types of girls early in my college career. Once they are spending their own money, it is surprising how fast they're looking for sales and cutting back on purchases.

As guys we don't have the separate types of clothing, we simply layer all of our summer clothing when it gets cold. The only piece of winter clothing you should really own is a winter coat, no creepy collection of scarves, mittens (glove that smell of oil are the only ones acceptable), sweaters, turtlenecks, or anything weird like that. You're not making a Christmas family album or giving your grandson little caramel candies so stop the creepy Grandpa wardrobe. People will assume you're foreign or a serial killer if you have a winter wardrobe.

Now from a guy's perspective girls that brands matter have told me. Going into college I did not realize that this was even issue because it was something that I rarely ran into in high school. I had heard about it from kids who transferred out of my high school to wealthier schools, but we usually just made fun of the kids who wore nice clothes back in the day. But these kids usually came from a rare rich family in the community, and certainly did not correlate with the majority of students who settled on Wal-Mart and Target clothing. This where I'll incorporate the help of my friends Christen and Brittany:

Athletic brands (Nike, Adidas, Reebok, Under Armour, etc.)

Christen: Definitely straight, doesn't try too hard, athletic, comfortable with himself, cool kid.

Brittany: Definitely straight and athletic. Confident, and doesn't need clothes to be flashy.

Tommy Hilfiger

Christen: Cares about what he looks like, meaning he cares that he's the one not buying it, and his mom or girlfriend is taking care of it.

Brittany: Straight guys, I like the cologne... it's a guy who likes the beach and comes from a family with a yacht.

Aeropostale

Christen: Definitely living in the past, very high school-feel, he probably used a fake to get in.

Brittany: Aero is a brand everyone wore in high school to be popular, but wasn't. Unless he had a gorgeous face, I wouldn't talk to him.

Lacoste

Christen: I wouldn't know a dude was wearing Lacoste unless he told me, and that's a problem.

Brittany: Is that the Alligator one?

Polo

Christen: This guy definitely has his act together, and looks good while doing it. I'm going to bet he smells amazing too.

Brittany: Mmmm, Yes sir! This guy would definitely get a call back.

American Eagle

Christen: A little nicer than Aero, but still kind of your average Joe guy.

Brittany: Same category as Aeropostale but a little better.

Old Navy

Christen: Yeeeah, I mean he's on a budget, and that's fine, but Old Navy board shorts really aren't going to catch my eye.

Brittany: Old Navy is a no-go.

Gap

Christen: Worn correctly, gap has potential. I still say that only aunts and grandma's shop for their nephews and grandsons there.

Brittany: Gap is okay. It reminds me of Gap Baby.

Ecko

Christen: Ecko is allll over the place. Indie? Punk? Hood? I don't even know. He's a little clothes-conscious for my taste, I'd say.

Brittany: Ecko reminds me of a hoodlum or a gangsta-hater. But after looking at the site, it could be a little metro.

Banana Republic

Christen: LOVE banana republic. Tasty!

Brittany: Classy and shows his well-off with good taste.

Calvin Klein

Christen: This is tricky, if he's wearing a t-shirt that says Calvin Klein, he's gay or trying way too hard. If he's dressed up wearing Calvin Klein then I feel like he's just a young-professional, has it together.

Brittany: This is when the clothes come off. I'm thinking underwear. He probably wears boxer-briefs. It's Victoria's Secret for men.

Perry Ellis

Christen: Ummm who? Boorrring!

Brittany: Seems kind of old-manish!

Georgio Armani

Christen: This is the time I start looking at prices of drinks. Chances are, I'm over my head! They better be buying!

Brittany: High class, is well-off, cares what he looks like, buys nice things.

Express

Christen: I love it when guys wear express. It kind of makes their sexuality ambiguous, but who cares? They look amazing and I could look all night!

Brittany: Kind of metro, business attire in a really nice way. Good taste!

True Religion

Christen: Very nice! Pretty pricey, but it looks good!

Brittany: Me likie!

You'll be working on a limited budget so I highly suggest using the Internet over going to the stores to pick up clothes. I have gotten slightly used shorts for 1/3 of the price of what they cost in the store by going on Ebay and after one wash in with the laundry you're in the game tricking girls into thinking you have more money than you do. You can get a bulk order of LaCoste and Polo shirts on the Internet at around $20-$25 a pop as in comparison to around $35-$40 in stores. I have been doing it for years, and growing progressively better at it. I had a sports card business on Ebay throughout my college days and learned how to use the site to my advantage when it came to the search engine. I shortly thereafter started find clothing and electronics at an extremely cheap price. In fact, I don't remember the last time I paid for a DVD, electronics, books, or clothing at full price.

You don't need to be flashy, because the d-bags have worn out that approach; you just need to look clean and appear as if you put in some sort of effort. Girls will eat this up faster than chocolates on Valentine's Day, because they notice subtle hints. We don't have the sense to notice nor care about subtle hints. We use those brain cells for sports and general beer knowledge. Eventually we'll pull a blind squirrel-acorn theory and some girl will fall into our trap of charm.

I think it is important to understand what items may confuse you as being someone you're not. More specifically, you want to dress to give an accurate portrayal of yourself and what you stand for. These items could be the Berlin Wall standing between you and girls wanting to talk to you. Leaving these items at home, or more important throwing them in the dumpster on your way out can be a social lifesaver.

Sweaters

The first items I would like to address are sweaters. Specifically the ones in the style close to a grandfather or Mr. Rogers I have seen trying to butt its way into society. Unless you are dressing up for a 2nd grade class photo, have pneumonia or are a sea captain these items are completely useless in the modern era. The only men who should be wearing sweaters are four year-olds whose mother dressed them for the Sears photo lab or 83 year-old men that feed pigeons in the park who could die at any moment if they contract a virus. You neither consistently golf at a country club nor do you run a Pittsburgh-based children's television show. Sweater vests are even pressing the issue to the point of absurd, to be safe toss that in the dumpster.

Crocs

Next we move on to Crocs. I feel it is only appropriate to wear Crocs if you're a kayaker, nurse, a pool cleaner or something involving lots of water. Otherwise you are a dumb ass, because I don't care how much you care about comfort you still look like a tool in those. It looks like a shoe a 4-year old came up with their art supplies. I can't believe that these are sold, and believe me people have tried to convince me to buy them.

I wouldn't wear those anti-girl magnets if they were my only option to running over burning lava. That's right; I would rather lose skin and flesh than look like an idiot with a pair of shoes made out of foam. At least I would be carried off on a stretcher with my pride in my pocket to know I'm still a man. I refuse to wear a shoe that hurts you when you try to stomp a pop can. These stupid contraptions are not an option, and any girl loses a point on the 1-10 hotness scale just by owning them. I can usually tell before I meet someone before I talk to them if they pop out of the car wearing these shoes of seemingly every color known to Crayola's color wheel.

Scarves

Scarves are only used if you are a serial strangler or planning to cut off circulation to a gunshot wound. I would much rather develop frostbite in the dead of winter than wear a scarf. You look like a Harry Potter, and we all know that he and all his fans are dorks (in a society where nerds seem to be becoming cool) so that nips that fashion bug in the butt. Scarves are just generally odd because it looks like you are hiding hickeys or some sort of weird rash. If someone rolls in from France and tries to pass one of these pieces of junk onto you, close the box and kindly ask for the receipt.

I can imagine the inventors of scarves sitting around a nice warm November fire. A wife is making a blanket, but she loses motivation only a fraction of the way in and decides that this six foot long jackass detector would be good for keeping your neck warm. Her husband laughed at her right in her face saying it was insane. But then she was able to trick the English, who we all know as the weirdest country in the world, into wearing these partially finished afghan blankets.

Foreign Hats

Any hat that is most likely seen in a foreign country, unless it is part of your religion, is a complete waste of money and your time. Weird French Suddam Hussein hats, creepy furry Soviet hats, baskets toting fruit, or anything that could be misconstrued as you being a pedophile is a no go unless it is Halloween. When Halloween rolls around you can pull out all stops and wear any goofy items you want. Sometimes I just wore items I collected from other people, with no real costume in mind to a person's place just to get free beer. One year I wore a straw hat, muscle shirt, and swimming trunks then claimed I was Mr. Summer Vacation. But weird hats any time other than Halloween is not all right, because you will probably show up on the convicted sex criminal website without even committing a crime. People will just assume that part of your sentencing was wearing a ridiculous cowboy hat with a feather on to flag that you're a rapist.

Jean Shorts

Jean shorts, especially the home made edition, are completely and totally out of line unless you're a 40 year-old man who plans to go on a boating trip in the middle of some hick town lake. Basically when you wear jean shorts, specifically homemade jean shorts, you are telling the world that there is no reason to impress anyone ever again. Jean shorts are like saying, "It's too hot to be normal and wear jeans, but I'm too broke to buy cargo shorts." Basically, you send out the completely wrong message to the crowd, and if you want to pick up overweight white trash women you've got the right gear on.

Do not wear anything NASCAR related for many of the same reasons why you don't wear jean shorts. You do not even have the common courtesy to support athletics, which NASCAR is far from being. As a former sports journalism major, we used to have to pull straws for who had to report on NASCAR news for the local yocals to hear. When you are wearing NASCAR items you're not even supporting an area that might tell a stranger something about you that could start up a great conversation. Generally, women will avoid you if come in wearing an M&M's jacket and a DuPont hat unless you are the driver of those cars yourself.

Sleeveless Shirts and Large Holed Jeans

Unless it is cowboy night at the bar and there is a large mechanical bull on the premises, you are just going to look like a piece of trash if you walk into a trendy bar with a sleeveless shirt. Furthermore, neither of these items should have any flammable liquids trapped in the threading. With all the cigarettes being lit up around a bar there is a good chance you will need to practice the stop, drop, and roll before going out. Besides do you really want a girl who is impressed by a guy who dresses like he traded outfits with a hobo that he just killed?

Off-colored hats or hats of teams you don't cheer for

Lastly, hats of teams you do not even cheer for or owning hats that are off-color from the team's colors make you look stupid. I don't care that your hat matches your shoes or your shirt, why are you wearing an aquamarine colored Yankees hat? You're not making a fashion statement; you're making yourself look like an idiot to exactly 92% of the community. The hat you wear should always be close in color to the team you cheer for, not camouflage or some neon color. Also hats that have every team's logo on it are equally as dumb.

I realize the team has 50 different variations of their hat out to try to turn a larger profit. They only do this because their retail people are smarter than the mindless morons blowing $25 per hat to buy off-colored hats. Also please bend the bill and take the sticker off so it at least looks like it fits comfortably. I know you're trying to be gangster or whatever showing that you have enough money to buy new extravagant hats, but you've just pooled a serious tool move.

A note about accessories:

Hats:

Christen: If a guy is a hat person, it goes a long way! Hats almost always add a little something something.

Brittany: I like it when guys wear hats and have them tipped to the side. Hats are very sexy.

Watches:

Christen: I LOVE when a guy is wearing a watch. Sooo much better than glancing at his cell phone

Brittany: I like expensive-looking watches! Shows he has a schedule!

Earrings:

Christen: Nope, I'm not into it. I wouldn't write a guy off for it, but if I say a guy, I'd assume he was a tool.

Brittany: Only a diamond stud. It just depends on the guy if he can have 2 or 1.

Facial piercings:

Christen: No again. I'm already afraid.

Brittany: No, unless he's Spanish.

Necklaces/Bracelets

Christen: "Mannery" is totally fine with me, as long as its not excessive. Pretty hot.

Brittany: It's good, as long as it's not excessive or costume-ish.

Shoes: (depends on situation)

Christen: I'm into dress shoes, but this is more getting ready for the post-college scene.

Brittany: I like Tim's, if he's wearing jeans. Sneakers are good too.

Be Responsible When You Drink

Coming back after a long night of drinking to the dorms is like surviving a major military battle. You will come back dirty with spills on you, sometimes carrying a guy up to the dorm, and not everyone makes it back. Some people get picked up for under age drinking and some are left at the scene of the skirmish on the couch or on the floor until the next morning. Those who do make it back tell tales of great times to be had to those still at home before jumping in the shower and settling in for a long night of pizza bagels and recovery.

First and foremost rule of surviving the world of drinking is you do not want to be an idiot and do stupid things that will get you in trouble with family, friends, and the law. When you start drinking you assume the responsibility for your actions because it was your choice to drink in the first place. Having a night out is a lot of fun but you run into people who shouldn't drink at all. They're usually the guys who punch holes in the dry wall and girls who can't stop crying and complaining about their lives. These people are an absolute waste to take out and should simply seek some mental help. Since you're not a psych major, they're not your problem.

You will find out fairly quickly who the people are that are no fun to drink with because it will make for many drama filled and awkward moments. They act out of emotions, and usually drink way too much too fast for their own good. They think drinking is a sprint, where it is actually a marathon that includes a mixture of food and a variety of drinks. You run into the idiots who do things like Jack Daniels or Vodka bongs and take years off their lives doing so. These are the tools that end up killing people because imitators think they can do the same thing.

One such occurrence happened during my junior year of college right around Halloween. I crossed a busy street to get over to my apartment to cook a pizza bagel and relax for the rest of the night with my roommates. I crossed the street and was walking to my apartment building to unlock the door and let myself in. All of a sudden, I hear what sounds like a deer smashing the hood of a car. I thought I was just hearing things until I got up the three flights of stairs that led up to my fourth floor apartment. When I looked down people on the street were freaking out.

A kid who had been drinking had sped through a green light and hit a couple kids crossing the street. Apparently, he knocked the kids right out of their shoes killing one and putting the other in a very long coma. These two kids had been drinking near a party where I had just come from and were hit no more than 45 seconds after I crossed at the same spot. To be somewhat fair, the kids who crossed did not do so at a crosswalk; but that still does not excuse the driver from what he did driving at allegedly almost twice the legal limit. It is a memory I'll never shake.

The entire block was shut down and three lives were destroyed because they all decided to do dumb things while drinking. I'm just glad it wasn't me; I have a gift of being very aware of my surroundings and not being a jerk when I drink. Actually most people can't even tell I'm drunk when I have been drinking because I act exactly the same way sober. This is skill has gotten me out of a number of tight situations, including the one I mentioned earlier during my sophomore year.

You don't want to be the guy that people are telling second hand stories about on Wednesday about your previous Friday night either. I have had friends that have done a great number of stupid things once they are intoxicated that I still laugh about to this day. There will be no shortage of acts that will be accomplished once drunk by you and your friends that you will tell for years. They will always be tough to remember off the top of your head, but once someone gets you going you will say "Oh, hey you remember that idiot who..."

I have just a few examples of things you don't want to do after you're been intoxicated. First and foremost, avoid blacking out and climbing dangerous things like trees and buildings that get you arrested. Don't yell at people in the streets, especially cops, because that is a great way to get pepper sprayed and arrested. Also don't pick fights, you'll probably get your butt kicked and subsequently arrested. Stealing or destroying property is another great way to end up in cuffs.

Superman Drunk

The balcony to our apartment was a setting of a close friend throwing a bed frame down to the parking lot at 2:30 AM late one night. It was a long night at the bar and he tended to love showing feats of strength whenever his beer muscles came out to play. In fact this friend once stole an old rusty bike from a rack on campus on the premise that he did not feel as bad if it was the worst bike on the rack. He lived a long ways from campus and took the bike home and left it in his yard.

Once this friend who is from Pittsburgh got tired of being yelled at and jeered every time he walked past this house of Philadelphia sports fans going to and from his apartments. I saw him standing by himself at a table in the bar we were at when he looked at me and said, "I'm going to do it." I had no idea what he was talking about, but he put a glass ashtray in his pocket and left the bar. I went on with my night as normal. I completely forgot about the whole situation until I got a text that said, "I did it, I threw the ash tray through their front living room window." It made me laugh and think now that is a comeback because it was March in a cold Pennsylvania winter.

He also once found a log used to keep dirt from sliding broken off one night on his walk home. He carried the log for four blocks until he got to his place and found no reason to keep it, and then tossed it in the middle of the street. Ironically, he threw it in front of a police car that did not stop to confront him, but instead swerved around it and kept going. Sometimes God is on your side I guess.

Finding a Toilet is Essential

First off, making it back to your bed is half the battle but once you get there that does not mean that the night is over. I have heard of people throwing up in their bed and peeing in their bed, or worse yet going over to someone else's place and peeing or puking their bed. One such old friend of mine had a girl over one school night, when my buddy woke up he had to go to an early class so he left the apartment. When he got back there was a note from the girl saying she spilled a cup of water in the bed. My friend threw off the covers to find a three-foot diameter yellow puddle in his bed, hardly a cup of water. He promptly threw the cover out on the balcony, but not to hide the urine stain he flew it like it was a flag of his native country.

In the same apartment, a freshman we knew that year showed up drunk out of his mind. Seth talked loudly for a while before passing out on the couch in the living room. Sometime later he had to go to the bathroom and peed all over the couch. The couch was never slept on again by people who knew of the incident because it smelled like a kennel; from that day on the couch was named after the kid who peed on it.

I once had a buddy Jim who slept in the top bunk of his dorm and rolled out one night to fall six feet. He just laid there and groaned, but apparently did not wake up because while laying there recovering, he peed the rug he was laying on. Still content to lay in urine for a long stretch, he later got up to go to the bathroom, but could not find it. He did find something almost as good by his drunken standards; it was an electrical socket in the wall. He gave it a good soaking much to the disgust of his roommate who woke up to him in the act. Luckily, he was not electrocuted.

Once on a spring break trip our friend got hammered drinking a 64-ounce Rum and Coke he made in a Gatorade bottle. He managed to finish the drink in less than an hour which got him raging up and down the beach talking to any girl he came across and snagging free beers as he went. Eventually we made it back to our hotel and convinced him to go to bed. After he was in bed for a while and we were relaxing he got up to go to the bathroom. Instead of going to the room's bathroom he walked over to the middle vanity drawer and started to relax. We all jumped out of our seats to tackle him and carry him to the bathroom, not because we knew the room would smell like urine for the rest of the trip, but because the Bible was in the drawer he was getting ready to go in. I felt like that maybe a ticket to hell for all of us in some way.

Another friend of ours was notorious for blacking out and getting up in the middle of the night to go odd places. One particular night he got up and stumbled around the apartment for a while before settling on a place to go. He ended up walking past his bathroom and back to his bedroom where he proceeded to urinate in his hamper. The next day he couldn't understand why all his dirty clothes were wet and smelled like pee, until he was reminded of the act.

To keep the urine jokes flowing, Jim is notorious for his peeing in random places. He once received a citation for peeing beside an ATM alongside a busy street in State College. Now public urination is not an uncommon thing at a place that has plenty of bars, believe me I've been to New Orleans and Bourbon Street is probably the most disgusting street I have ever been on. This is coming from a guy who has been on spring break to Panama City Beach and walked The Strip in Las Vegas multiple times. Beaver Avenue in State College can be thrown in as one of the grossest streets in North America, but boy is it fun from Thursday to Saturday.

To make a long story short, and no that was not a perverted reference; my friend got a citation for public urination. He kept making fun of the officer who was writing him up and warned other people that the area was not safe to urinate in because he got the maximum fine. But this isn't uncommon I wouldn't even want to know how many citations are handed out for public urination on college campuses per year. All I know is over time you will learn to pinpoint squad cars from 100 yards away and even undercover cars with their high-tech antennas. You will also learn of safe spots to publicly urinate. I'm not recommending you do this, but sometimes you don't have a choice when your kidneys burst.

Making Food

In another instance, a friend of ours came back smashed out of his mind and decided he wanted to make a sandwich. So he got out all the makings for a turkey sandwich out of the refrigerator and set them on the counter and started to calmly make a sandwich. He was stumbling throughout the process, but everyone looked onward from the couch and saw him concentrating very hard on what he was doing. He started to make his way across the living room but passed out during the walk and spilled the sandwich all over the floor in his fall. What was found still shocks and amazes me. He had put a pack of sticky notes on the sandwich instead of cheese.

This is just a story of an example of what the alcohol will do to your body. It demands food, preferably greasy food that you might not normally eat in daily sober life. I wouldn't recommend cooking anything elaborate if you go against going to a restaurant and eating something at home. The last thing you want to do is start a kitchen fire like some sort of idiot because you thought you could make a Denver omelet. You always think you're smarter than you are when you're drunk.

I Should Have Stopped Drinking Infinity Drinks Ago

I have a friend (who ended up later being a roommate) who during his freshman year used to get ridiculously drunk and end up weird places. One time, my former dorm neighbor and this friend were taking the long walk back from an apartment complex back to the dorm. When they got to the baseball field, my future roommate decided he couldn't make it any farther and sat in the dugout to take a rest. My neighbor sat down next to him, but after a few minutes my friend decided he needed to go to sleep so he stretched out in the visitor's dugout for the night. My neighbor had to practically drag him from the dugout to our dorm, which was just another couple hundred yards away.

I once opened my door to find this same kid asleep in the hallway. I grabbed his ankles and drug him inside my room and grabbed his bottle of cheap vodka next to him and brought it in as well. I mean that is what friends are for. They are for keeping your buddies out of cuffs.

This same friend used to take his pants off at parties, but would be wearing basketball shorts under his jeans. We would rarely see him take the pants off, but it was always the sure sign that he was wasted when you would pass him in the room carrying his folded up jeans in one hand and a drink in the other. Despite the risks to his health, that was our favorite era of for all those who surrounded him. We still loved him even though I once caught him trying to take a shot of Tide that I had to knock out of his hand like a little kid drinking things from under the sink.

One such story that comes to my mind for him is after a night at a local bar where we were going head-to-head drinking Long Island Ice Teas. Needless to say after a while we were pretty gone, so we started walking home on a blistery winter night. When we got back, I went to the bathroom and came back out into the living room to find him half inside the apartment and the top half of his body outside on our balcony with a keg that we still had from a previous party. I asked him to come inside; he said, "No, leave me and save yourself!"

Knowing that I couldn't leave him out there or he'll get pneumonia I convinced him to at least wiggle inside so I could close the door, which he agreed to do. Once inside, I asked him to go to bed for which he offered me a deal:

"I will only go to bed if you go into your room, close the door, and do not watch me go to bed."

I laughed at the request and agreed, but admittedly I peeked through the crack of my cheap bedroom door to see him stumbling into his room. In the process, he walked straight into his door and did some sort of spin move to fall into his room and flat on his face. The door then went shut. Since he woke up the next afternoon, he lived through the night.

Drinking is like a Hot Bath; You Ease Yourself In

I've had my own embarrassing stories involving having too much to drink. I once passed out in the middle of a party and had a two-foot long penis drawn the majority of the length of my arm leading down to my hand. That took two days to come off as I wore a long sleeve shirt or a hooded sweatshirt throughout the process of removal. But there was one story that is much worse than the male genitalia being drawn on you.

During my freshmen year at Penn State-Altoona, we did not have a great deal going on one Friday night so a friend spoke up saying that we could go to a friend's farm house. We all looked at each other and agreed to do that, so booze and other necessities were loaded for the 90-minute trek east. We made a stop to pick up a couple of kids from main campus (University Park) and continued on. When we got there the door would not open and the key was jammed.

We put our friend (who is about 5'6") into a firewood loading dock and he was able to open the door to a spot beside the fireplace and walk over to unlock the door. After that, the night really took off with shots of cheap vodka that still sends shivers up my spine to this day. After a good number of those we started playing a power hour in the living room, which had some sort of lighthouse theme. Once we got through that, those of us still left standing attacked the beer bong and at this point I lost my shirt. Somewhere in the physical universe we occupy exists a picture of me with a 5-foot long snake pillow shirtless taking my first beer bong.

When the night started winding down and people were passing out throughout the house, I would be comfortable to say I was the most lit. I found a comfortable spot on a hard wood floor for a while, until someone told me to turn down the music. I was ten feet away from the speaker I just tried to reach out for the knob to turn it, but when I realized I didn't have go-go gadget arms I fell back to the ground. Someone else walked the length of the house to turn it down instead.

After a short while I started feeling sick, so I ran for the door to the patio. When I went to the side of the porch to throw up I fell forward and quickly realized it was an elevated deck. I grabbed a patio couch on the way down and ripped that down with me in the process. I'd imagine those watching inside had a great laugh because all they saw was my hands coming over the deck side and doing a pull-up to get back inside. It didn't help that it was March and 35 degrees with a driving rain storm outside.

I got back inside and lay back on the floor and passed out under some other kid's jacket while others lay comfortably in other parts of the house. Apparently, after I passed out my friend Jim was running around buck naked throughout the house to creep out the others. I thank God every day that I was not conscience to see the spectacle. But I saw many others that made me sick later on in my college career.

The following day while recovering from what would be one of the greatest hangovers of my life. I had to sit in a car with the kid we put in the wood feeder for 90 minutes, which I know doesn't sound bad. But this kid used to treat a common trip across town like it was an Indy Car race with lots of abrupt stops and accelerations, really putting Newton's Laws to the test. Besides that he always had the heat on in the car and was usually smoking a cigarette. We loved this kid but were deathly afraid of riding in a car with him. My very weak stomach was enduring G-forces that I'm not sure it could replicate in this lifetime.

The entire ride we were stopping and starting as I was in the passenger's seat sweating like I was working in a steel mill. What made it worse was that it was 35 degrees outside and raining so I couldn't put the window down to get out the smoke or heat. I'm pretty sure I was still drunk when I got to my dorm at 2 PM the next day; quite an accomplishment for such a long drive where my shirt was soaked through. I lived on a steady diet of Spaghettios the rest of the weekend.

The Drunken Dial/Text

Electronics are a dangerous thing whenever you have been drinking. Your true emotions start to come out and you want to talk to everyone; so what two items do you rely on most to communicate? The telephone and the computer, and both can me lethal whenever you have been drinking. I used to be a drunk text violator and I would message people on AOL Instant Messenger to have a real in depth conversation.

Does anyone still use that? Accept while intoxicated you usually allude to more information than you would ever want to let out.

You don't want to text or message someone something embarrassing like you peed your pants because you couldn't make it all the way home. These are the types of messages you certainly want to "x" out of and not backtrack the next morning to see what you text. You will simply cringe at the damage you inflict. You hammered with technology at your hands is like giving a drunk the control of a wrecking ball, without the death and tearing down buildings, unless your life was a metaphorical building, of course.

I personally like to get on sites like "Texts from last night" and "FML" just to read the things people are talking about. But do you really want to be the subject of others amusement? Those sites are genius because thousands see what booze and electronics lead to. Alcohol makes you push your phone's capabilities.

I have friends that will go through their phone for every available single girl they find attractive to try to get them to come hang out. They just want to get the hook up, but don't use the correct format to attack that cause. The problem is that the drunk guy usually will text multiple girls, and somehow to your amazement the girls know each other. You may even be stupid enough to text two girls that live together and go for the grail, but you'll probably just pass out alone that night.

The quicker that you can forget about messaging and texting while intoxicated the better your life will be. You don't want to have to go through and spend half of the next day apologizing for inappropriate statements to people the night before. You will even try calling people you haven't even talked to in years, also not realizing you are doing so at 1 AM. Drunk is apparently its own timezone. But the worst stories are sending inappropriate texts to the wrong people. I've heard a couple stories about someone sending "Do you want to make out?" text messages to their parent's phones.

Girls also have a very short lifespan for their phones as in comparison to guys. I can't go a week without a girl sending me something about giving them my number because their phone fell in the toilet, a pond, or miraculously smashed against a wall. That or you could be my friend who had a bowl of soup in one hand and his phone in the other. After about a minute of holding the soup in his hand, he realized the phone was cooking in his microwave.

We're All Idiots On Occasion

The police are knocking at my dorm room door. My roommate is stumbling all over the place pleading with me not to answer. I'm a 20-year-old sophomore in college and panic ensues. I had eight beers that night with my neighbor. I try to contain my fear and stay composed with my best poker face drawn. I calmly open the door and address the officers who have been called by the hall director because of my roommate's behavior. I act like a duck on water for the officers, calm on the outside but kicking and frantic on the inside. This is what true pressure is all about.

There is a male and female officer from the campus police, who happen to double as the real police on campus. These are not Mickey Mouse and Donald Duck cops; they can put you away if they so choose. Standing there I could tell this was routine for them. But tonight, it is me that all the onlookers are staring at and watching for some drama in their everyday boring lives.

I had thought it was going to be a relaxing night watching television in my room with a friend. But that night my roommate had decided it was a good idea to go shot for shot with a 6'7" 225 pound friend of ours. This was not an unusual practice, but my roommate was 5'7" 140 pounds and certainly no match for 12 shots of 100 proof Southern Comfort in an hour's time.

Earlier in the night, my neighbor came in and wanted to watch a college basketball game with me. I decided to take the night off because I was tired and had some schoolwork to do, which obviously did not get finished that night. He knew that I had gotten a case of Miller High Life for $10 on special, which is terrific price any time, even more so for a 20 year old kid who was still new to drinking. My neighbor threw me $5 and the drinking began as we rooted for Duke University in a classic ACC match up with North Carolina. By the end of the game my neighbor had kicked nine brews and I finished eight. Not exactly a bad pace for a two-hour game.

I remember thinking that the craziest nights always start calm. Life takes a crazy twist when you least expect it and you can never quite prepare yourself for it. You have to sit back and roll with the punches, praying that everything works out just the way you have planned. I am not one for planning ahead, so rolling with the punches has never really been a problem for me. Tonight was just another crazy night in the life of a college sophomore.

My neighbor left and I decided to take it easy, a girl friend of mine came over. This was not unusual because she came over on a regular basis because my roommates and I always had a good time picking on one another and having fun. We were the type of guys you wanted to know in the dorms because we always provided entertainment for our friends. We were certainly the guys who could keep a smile on your face even on the worst of days.

After a while I heard a knock at the door. When I opened the door my roommate is standing in the doorway holding part of his front tooth and a pack of Camels. Apparently after drinking the 12 shots he decided to walk up the hill to an apartment just off our campus and along the way decided partake in a boxing match. Theme parties were standard during our time there, but a boxing match party was something I had not seen since I was in high school. Even then they were held in someone's barn or a field, not in a living room surrounded by dozens of people.

My roommate was drunk at a level we like to call "time traveling" or "blacked out" and he challenged a well-built, athletic kid in the room to fight. My roommate called him out by saying "I want you! You!" much like Carl Weathers playing the role of Apollo Creed in Rocky IV, one of our dorm room favorites. From second hand accounts I found out that the fight was over faster than a fat girl's stint in a game of dodge ball, with my roommate getting dropped by the more athletic opponent. Luckily, he collected his capped tooth in a zip lock bag to take home with him for a future dental project.

After having a few more beers, my roommate decided to walk down to our room in the dorms. He got in the building just fine and no one stopped him when he showed up at our room where my girl friend and I were hanging out. The girl who was visiting me and I got him convinced to get ready for bed and to lie down. I believed it was no big deal that particular night, but like I said the calmest nights are the ones you should fear the most.

Following some compromise, my roommate went to bed. I went out to sit on the couch in the TV lounge about 15 yards from my door to take in what just happened and laugh about it.

In this dorm, it was a suite set up and girls could live next to you or across the hall from your suite. This was really nice especially if you're a guy trying to add to your little black book. It was a refreshing change from freshmen year when we were trapped with all guys using a communal bathroom. I hated communal bathrooms after it took me a month to hack off planter's warts off my big toe following my freshman year.

As I'm relaxing out in the lounge and talking to some friends, my roommate tears into the room, yelling at me that he needs to smoke a cigarette and call his girlfriend. I told him to be a careful because I knew the R.A. to be a strict kid who was sheltered growing up. A strict college R.A. is the worst because they take the whole "mom when you're away from your mom" thing far too seriously. You want to kick their butt all the time but there are laws against such acts. Lucky for him.

About 10 minutes later, I see my roommate running at full speed from the R.A. sternly looking to catch him. I was mentioning following down the hall actually gaining on him while walking at a normal pace. My roommate had a frantic look on his face and he kept yelling "we need to take cover in the bunker!" The only problem with the whole scene was my roommate was running full speed propped up against the wall. If you have ever stepped foot in a physics classroom you understand the element of friction and my roommate's right side was taking the brunt of it.

My roommate went into the room and locked the door thinking that would save him. The R.A. came over to me and asked if I was his roommate, which I responded with a nod and told him not to worry about my roommate's behavior. The R.A. claimed he saw my roommate fall up the stairs on the way to our 3rd room suite, an observation I would not doubt happened. I told the R.A. it was no big deal and that my roommate planned on going to sleep and he has come back much worse shape. Assured that he had fulfilled his duty, the R.A. took off for his post in the downstairs lobby.

After about 20 minutes of being in our room with my roommate getting himself ready again for bed, he decided it would be a good idea to throw up in our bathroom so he would not feel sick the next day. This is a method taken by a lot of college students after a night of drinking got a little out of control. He went into our stall and pulled the trigger, and at that instant I heard a knock at the door. I opened the door thinking it was the girl I had been hanging out with that night. When I opened the door, greeting me was the 30-year-old overweight hall director and the R.A. who I calmed down. My roommate walked out of the stall, apparently feeling much better.

The hall director told me that he was obligated to call the police to come to the room because my roommate had obviously just thrown up. I agreed to let them come but first needed to shut the door so my roommate could change into his clothes, which the hall director allowed. While the door was shut I told my roommate to get dressed so he would be presentable. Meanwhile, I took all my remaining beers and put them in a cardboard 12 pack container of root beer I had. I then turned the 12 pack in my closet so it appeared as if it was simply an unopened half case of pop.

The remaining two or three beers that did not fit in I quietly walked over to my suitemate's room and to dump into the drawer of one of the desks. I took a swig of mouthwash and not more than a minute later I heard another knock at my door. I looked over to see my roommate dressed and ready to face the officers. I took a deep breath and opened the door.

I answered the door of my room to see the two officers looking at me with the building director and R.A. who turned my friend in standing behind. The officers walked in to talk to my roommate and search the room for any other alcohol. I am standing there sweating bullets hoping they do not search in my closet and discover the treasure chest of High Life cans I stashed in the backside of the root beer case. They walked past it at least a dozen times. I was a genius!

The girl who I had been hanging out with the whole night came in and out of the corner of her eye noticed an empty beer can on my desk. The officers had not made it that far into the dorm room and she took the can and threw it in my drawer. It must have been an empty can my neighbor left sitting at my desk while on my computer during the game. I looked around to see no signs of any other alcohol giving me a temporary sense of relief. Eventually, the officers took my girl friend and I out of the room to administer a sobriety test to my roommate in private. I thanked her for coming over and asked her to go back to her room, mainly to protect her because she had also been drinking that night.

The other officer took me out into the hall and started questioning me. They asked if I had been drinking that night; this is when the sweat really started brewing but I kept my cool. I told them I was about to go to bed when this fiasco started. I knew darn well it was better to lie with the poise I have been blessed with that comes through even when drinking. To look even more composed I kept asking questions about what will happen to my roommate, what they needed me to do, should we come with him, and a bunch of other questions. I firmly believe I sweated out all the alcohol in my system in about a 10-minute conversation.

The door to my room opened back up and they said they had to take my roommate away because he blew over a certain number that requires an ambulance ride to the hospital. I said it wasn't a problem; the only problem was that my roommate had walked up and down the stairs many times that night without injury and now they wanted him to be taken out on a stretcher. I thought this was embarrassing so I tried to argue that I could just walk him down to avoid the onlookers. But I was unable to keep him from looking like a spectacle rolling down the hallway towards the elevator by paramedics.

We did follow him to the hospital to find out he was fighting the doctors who were trying to pump his stomach. We were at the hospital until 4:30 AM until I got back to go to bed for my 9 AM class, which I was absolutely wrecked for. I can't even begin to recall what happened in the class that seemed like an out of body experience. I was more concerned about going to pick my buddy up and hear his side of the story than I was about German culture.

Following class, my girlfriend and I drove back over to the hospital to get my roommate. He came out of the front doors in his bare feet because they hadn't allowed me to give them his shoes when he left for the night. He had peed his pants during the night because they didn't allow him to get up and go to the bathroom because he had to remain stationary until a certain hour. Still he greeted us with a big toothless grin and a wave as we rolled into the parking lot.

He was more concerned about his parents finding out about his chipped tooth than he was about the ticket for underage drinking that he had just received. He called and asked his cousin check the mail daily for the letter and bill that would go home from the university and the hospital. The $500 for a two-mile ambulance ride almost wiped out his entire checking account. To this day his parents never found out about the charge, which is a good thing for all of those involved.

We had many good times the rest of the year, but that one bonehead night was one of the dumbest things that ever could have happened to us. We really learned how dangerous alcohol was that night. But years later I look at it as another great story to tell girls and friends at the bar where I can now legally drink.

Where You'll Probably Be Partying: Year by Year Analysis

Before you even start college you may have been lucky enough to be from a community that had enough money to allow kids to party. Congratulations jerk, I did not come from such a community. Our ideas of a party was going out to a barn and have guys box each other while people rounded up what booze they could find and drank in the nearby field; hardly a social function to speak of. It sounds more like a 1930's speakeasy than it does a high school party.

You will follow a distinct pattern of places to party that most kids follow throughout their progression of college. Really you work up the social scale from the early fraternity parties and then start going to classier bars by the time you leave as you have become mature and developed your tastes. Besides the taste you find out a lot about yourself such as favorite drinks, where they're cheapest and what type of environment you enjoy.

During your freshmen year you will have a higher degree of desperation of where to party. You won't know much of anyone, and will actually spend a great deal of nights sitting around trying to find something to do. Fraternities will be attacking you to rush like you're the hottest college football recruit in the country, it will be annoying but eventually you will get passed it. However, you may milk them for the alcohol a few times by saying you are thinking about rushing to the house.

Most people rush to fraternities before they know what is all out there. Before they know it they're running in their boxers through the quad and giving another guy some sort of weird social handshake that non-members can't know. You will start rattling off the Greek alphabet in the assumption that other non-Greeks give a damn or envy you. Don't worry about it, because we don't. I would say go to a handful of fraternity parties because some nights they maybe your only option.

You probably won't know a great deal of upperclassmen in apartments or ones that will buy you alcohol so fraternities are one known safe source. The problem is unless you say you're rushing or you have tons of great looking girls with you then they won't let you in. They always have some douche bag working at the door asking you who you know like he's working the backstage access at a KISS concert. He won't be the biggest ass that lives in the house, but he most likely will be the biggest and dumbest. Little does he know that he will probably be peaking professionally right where he is.

Getting alcohol as a freshman is really at a premium because it is rare. Good-looking girls, as you've learned, can get anything they want because guys who are 21 and still awkward around girls will agree to buy them alcohol. They maybe even dumb enough to pay for it themselves just so he feels that he can hang out with the girls. He thinks he has a chance, but I've got news; he will have a snowball's chance in hell with those girls. They are just using him for his age to get drunk on good alcohol, and then go flirt with some tool at the party with a diamond stud earring.

It will be important to try to convince these girls to come out with you to a party. Anytime you roll into a party uninvited with a disproportionate number of guys over girls, people will look at you like you have the plague. If you're rolling six guys deep with no girls, you might as well stay home watching movies and playing video games. It will be far more productive than anything you'll experience that night and whole lot less frustrating. But you need to gather a large amount of girls' numbers early on and keep calling them up from time to time to keep in contact and hopefully get you something to do.

I don't think people understand the struggle that freshmen guys go through in the pursuit to have a good time. They are at the bottom of the social totem pole because they can't buy alcohol, don't have an apartment, haven't develop college street smarts and still don't have a large network of friends. Guys like to hang out with freshmen girls because they haven't added the dreaded freshmen 15 yet and they're still naive. In contrast, upperclassmen girls don't like to hang out with freshmen guys because they haven't filled out and they are still awkward. It is like a slap in the face, because you won't get invited to parties but the girls you know will have 3 or 4 places to choose from.

If you have the opportunity to get beer or alcohol as a freshman, take advantage of it. The chances to get booze early on will be few and far between, but you can't be a glutton. Odds are, whoever is buying the alcohol is probably buying for more than just you. This predicament ushers in the dreaded quality vs. quantity argument. Simply, should you get quality alcohol or get more alcohol at a cheaper price? I highly suggest going for quality, but not top shelf stuff like Grey Goose or Patron. Ask for a bottle or case that is somewhere between $15-$25, because it will be quality but it won't be obvious you're showing off. Then share it only with close friends and people who could potentially hook you up with a great deal of fun like the cute girls getting into parties. But don't let her bring some tool shed guy to drink your booze before he goes out and tries to hook up with the girl. Developing close friends is vital.

Don't worry, you will start making friends throughout classes and activities on campus, you might even break into the big leagues early getting a handful of invitations to apartment parties. Once you get through the lies of telling fraternities you are rushing you probably won't go anymore unless you have a close friend who invites you to a random party. From here on out your parties will most likely be at apartment complexes. This will usher in sophomore year.

You still won't be old enough to buy alcohol on your own, but you have a year under your belt to meet people and friends will be moving into apartments. This is a year that can go either way with you living in the dorms or in an apartment. But if you live in an apartment, expect dorm friends to want to come over for a place to drink or crash after a long night of partying. The great part is you will probably have a handful of friends who are 21 and you're close enough with that will buy booze for you as long as you don't make it a ridiculous order.

If you live in the dorms, you will need a backpack and possibly something that is soft and can buffer noise to sneak bottles into your dorm. I did this my first two years and was never stopped once. In fact, I had to do it in graduate school because the extreme Baptist lifestyle does not allow alcohol, not even to 23-year-old graduate students. I used to jam my backpack like the old days and walk in to store my fridge with icy cold refreshments to enjoy after coming home from class.

Your life as a sophomore will be almost exclusively apartment parties. You will still be a little on edge about being busted for an underage, so you will be cautious and putting on an act when you pass RA's and policemen on your way home. They honestly don't give a damn unless you're peeing all over the place, vomiting, or acting in an outrageous manner. They understand because they drank back in the day just like you are now, plus it looks pretty sketchy when you're wearing a backpack at 11:30 on a Saturday night. I have actually had a beer with apartment security on several occasions.

You will have a good idea about campus, how strict it is and handling yourself not to get busted by the end of your sophomore. You will also start getting sick of all the cheap plastic bottle liquor and bottom shelf beer that you get at apartment parties and fraternity parties. But the tables have turned because you are the guys who are talking to the freshmen girls and inviting them places, then screwing over the guys who were you last year. It is the natural order of how college partying works, someone has to get screwed and that someone is always freshmen guys.

All right, next comes junior year and you're still rocking out at apartments. But now the apartments are better because most of your friends have made the transition from dorm to apartment. You will probably have multiple engagements to go to in any given night, and not many people are 21 yet. Those people who lived in apartments the previous year are back in their place or they have upgraded to a better quality location. But as the year goes on a threat looms.

People start turning 21 and bars become a viable option as in comparison to apartment parties. You look more sophisticated and grown up at the bar and you don't have a mess to clean up whenever everyone is gone the next morning. You can always get whatever drink you want and the environment in most cases is better than anything you encounter at an apartment party. But apartment parties still remain fairly strong because people's birthdays are all spread out. Remember you still have sophomore friends who are 19 and 20 coming to your parties as well, so the parties are still pretty banging. I would say junior year is the best year overall for partying.

I remember many of our parties were around 75-100 people there at any given time. The fire marshal only allows 20 at a place our size at any given time, but the apartment building knows you will throw parties anyways. We had a top floor place, which made the balcony a popular place as well. But as the year went on our parties, although still popular, were slowly trickling numbers. As you get older you gain more friends, thus more social responsibilities and not as many people were hanging around for 2-4 hours at your place. But bars will become more attractive and you start leaking friends to bars because they don't have to Barry Sanders it (finding holes in the defense) to the keg anymore. You now feel like a creep going to meet freshmen and invite them over to hang out, so there is no replacement to the friends who choose the bar over your place.

Then comes senior year and most of your friends have turned 21 and realize that jumping from bar to bar is the perfect thing to do. Parties turn into strictly a 45-minute pre-game period before the club or bar with all the liquor you used to previously hide. Before when you threw parties you knew the "Rogue Beer Thief" would be there to snatch liquor if it was available. Nothing pisses you off more than someone who is invited to your place, drinks your beer, and then also steals items while they're there.

You only throw small gatherings of close friends and girls you are working on for the pre-game session, which is accompanied by tunes. You will need to talk as wingmen about the plan for the night, while your girls will be talking about important life issues they have somewhere else in the apartment. After about 4-6 shots or three or four mixed drinks you'll be ready to go just in time to beat the cover charge at your destinations and in time for specials. You will probably be doing this two or three time a week and having a blast doing so. Remember, the working world is not as accepting of this lifestyle so live it up.

Eventually your bank account, body, and grades will take a small hit and you need to start slowing down. But you press forward, know that these are the last great party days you will have with your closest friends. You will even go to the occasional apartment party still to visit friends and say hi. Don't worry, you'll snag a shot or two and also a beer while you're there, but it is simply a side stop for whatever bar you will be going that night.

By the end of the year, you will start getting short on money and you will be tired from all the grind of college classes and social life. Some of your weaker friends will actually be looking forward to graduating from college, but they will reverse that thought after about a month of living in some tiny bumble of a town. People will not go out nearly as much your last semester, but will instead save the money for spring break and senior week around graduation time. The body will take a month to re-cooperate from both experiences, and although you black out you will never forget the fun you have. Worst case scenario is that you're tagged with the pictures the next day.

Then there are the people who defy the norm of joining the work force and go to graduate school. They will shortly find out that it is much more difficult than undergraduate life was. You will be regressing even farther from the party lifestyle because of a lack of time and a commitment to jobs and graduate assistant ship work on top of the school workload. You may only go out once or twice if you're lucky during the week. You probably won't get as ridiculously drunk when you do go out because you have to get up early to do some 30 page reading and evaluation of the text the next day.

But you'll still make the random appearance at an apartment party or two of friends who were younger than you. The problem is you don't know as many people because most of your friends have moved on despite you continuing to live the dream. You will grow tighter with friends that you still have left at the school, and with some of your new graduate school friends. The new friends won't be able to fill the void of former friends who you have deep-rooted relationships with, but they will do a decent job because you realize you mean the same to them. There will be more dinner outings and fancier bar trips than anything. You are preparing for adulthood, and adulthood sucks. Keep living the dream as long as possible. But to say that college is the best four years of your life is crazy. It just sets up better days down the road.

Parties

CAUTION: DON'T BE AN IDIOT WHEN YOU DRINK. I KNOW PLENTY OF THEM, I DON'T NEED MORE.

I think it is important to emphasize safety at a party, especially with fire. I have hosted and been to a good number of parties where fire has been brought out in the form of flaming Dr. Peppers, lighting fireworks in the middle of a busy street, lighting a balcony on fire with Everclear, setting Cacti on fire, and just general lighter salutes when Free Bird comes onto the play list. You would be surprised how many things are flammable in an apartment soaked in alcohol. Seeing that you will likely have 4-5 times the legal limit of people allowed in your apartment, flames are a bad idea.

Great, now that we have confronted fire we can move onto the point of a party, having a good time. You should have certain goals going into a party because now with the onset of Facebook events you can tell who will be going to this shindig days in advance. You can tell if it will be a brodeo, a good number of friends, lots of cute girls, or just a general mixture. This is not something I had a freshman, because Facebook events had not broken soil yet, or cyber world soil, so to speak.

While going to a party you have to understand getting to the keg is a premium because these tiny apartments will have a lot of people in them so make every trip to the keg worth it. The keg will invariably be placed in a corner or some inaccessible location. Also parties will give you a level of credibility with the girls there seeing that you have a lot of mutual friends and aren't afraid to drop a little bank. It'll earn you points with the girls, and also the new girls that come to your place because you'll have a common friend link. Don't underestimate the common friend, because it gives you instant line of credibility and a source to come to when talking to the girl.

It is pretty much an unwritten rule that if you go over to other people's place the drinks must be free. Also an unwritten rule is not to charge people when they come into drink not only because it is against the law, but because you'll look like a jerk and people will remember you charging them. If anything, have a donation jar somewhere in the apartment and pass it around during the party a couple times then put it away. I have been to some people's parties that charge, but most have been for good causes or a charity. As a guy be prepared to pay more though.

A pretty good rule to live by when throwing a party is for you to have some type of fruity mixed drink you make in bulk for girls and kegs for guys. You'll need a keg for about every 40-50 people you expect to show up at the party. One large plastic container of mixed drink or two water coolers of mixed drink for the girls is sufficient enough to get you by for the night. This is a pretty good ratio to keep a party going for a few hours; but this is only a rule I would use for freshmen-junior years. In contrast, when you're a senior people usually only stick around for a drink or two and say hi, then leave. So a keg for every 55-60 that show is pretty standard. Also don't be an idiot by getting something fancy; I wouldn't spend anymore than about $60-$70 per keg. Honestly, most people don't care what type you get as long as it's free.

You will probably have people you do not even know coming into your party, take note of the dick weeds who invite a bunch of guys you do not know. Don't be that guy showing up with five guys tagging behind you to a party and which you were the only one invited. It is just bad karma; the most you can get away with is maybe two extra guys. But they better not be socially awkward either.

When one of these people throw a party, make a note of inviting a bunch of your guy friends who they don't know; fair is fair in the game of partying. You never bring a group of guys to a party because if you are lucky enough to even make it inside people will look at you the way little kids look at unwrapping a pair of socks during Christmas. No one wants them there and they are unwelcome. I do not care how cool you think you are and watch them do it on Entourage. I find it doubtful any of you are movie stars. Keep the number of guys and girls somewhat equal when you come to the party.

An instance that may kill you later is girls love to have conferences in the bathroom during a party. Did someone pack a large table in their purse because they couldn't finish business at the Holiday Inn Conference Center? I never really knew what was going on in there or if anyone was actually going to the bathroom. All I know is it ticks off everyone at the party who has to go to the bathroom because they will be in there for 20 minutes. Do they have a dry erase board calling out plays, and exactly how many girls are in there? Will there be a power point about how to better milk attention out of the guys at the party?

You will be pressed to the limits of your kidneys going into Def-Con four and launching nuclear missiles before these girls come out with this highly complex plan on how to attack the party. You will consider peeing in a cup, the stairwell, and ultimately what you will settle on if you don't make it is off the balcony. You will need someone running blocker like Smokey and the Bandit protecting each other from the cops. There is just something about peeing off a high elevation that is extraordinary to men. I believe it is trying to hit distant targets from a sizable height. It's almost like the water gun and balloon game at carnivals. But speaking of games you'll be faced with a variety of drinking games at parties.

There really only are about six party drinking games you should know; seven if you count a power hour pre-game session. If anyone else tries to bring games to the forefront it is completely unnecessary because these six games I am about to tell you about have been staples on college campuses for years. But you always have the random guy from some other college campus who believes he is in from some elite drinking platoon and has to teach dead asses how to drink. This guy is a tool and needs to shut up because his game is most likely awful and will take 15-20 minute of valuable pre-game time away explaining it.

First Game: Beer Pong

For those that don't know what it is, you will likely find out soon. It is a game that needs two ping pong balls, a long table and a stack of cups. It is fun and you pump through beer quickly because of it. Each time an opponent sinks a ball in your cup, you drink its contents. What a novel and great idea!

This is the game most college kids are familiar with and depending where you are you will find different variations and approaches to the game. Is bouncing allowed or not? How many times can we change the formation? Six or 10 cups? What happens if we shut out the other team? If the ball returns to me can I throw it behind my back? Is the game over if I sink it into the cup you are drinking from? All valid questions depending on where you are, but these set of rules are the ones I have run into most living both in the north and the south:

Depending on the size of the party determines if you play with six cups or 10. Good etiquette says if there is a monster list of people waiting to get into the game you play with six, and for health purposes you play with water in the cups so that you don't tick off the hosts by constantly changing the cups in and out. You instead drink from your own cup every time the other team sinks a ping-pong ball. However, if it is a small gathering it is acceptable to put beer into the cups that are in play and to play with 10 cups.

The general rule is that you can bounce at any table and if you get one to sink into a cup, then your opponents have to take two cups away and each take a drink. You have to be careful with this rule because once the ball makes contact with any surface and it can be batted away by your opponents out of defense. Also you want to take into account the material used for the pong table, which is usually wood. Occasionally you will run into a metal or plastic material, which is poor for bouncing.

Every now and then you have a shot that turns into a physic centrifugal force experiment where the ball is rolling around the rim like a Harlem Globe Trotter trick shot. In this case, only a girl who is present on the opposing team is allowed to blow the ball out of the cup, but may in no way physically touch the cup or the ball. In my experience I always get a drunk girl who thinks she can do swat the ball out of the cup like a grizzly bear and ends up knocking over half of our remaining cups; bottoms up for me.

Also with the six-cup formation it is generally accepted that you can only re-rack the cups once. There are various approaches people like to take. Some like the early re-rack of five cups pointed in a straight line back at the throwers known as the long and handsome. With four cups left, the most popular option involves a diamond formation, that still yields a large target but it is much tighter than that of the long and handsome straight-line approach. With three cups you have a couple of options; you can go with the Power-I (three cup variation of the long and handsome) or go with the mini-triangle, which is simply one cup in the front row and two in the back. Finally, the two-cup variation is usually a mini-I with one cup lined in front of the other.

If the occasion arises that you are shut out (opponent's rack is full while all your cups are gone) there are usually two consequences depending on where you are. You can either call your parents, regardless of the hour, and tell them you got shut out playing beer pong or you can streak. With the streaking option the location also has rules of either underwear or nude running down the highway or through the house following the embarrassing loss. Luckily, in my five years I was never shut out, I only shut out someone three or four times in the same five-year time span. Most times my opponent went for the calling their parents option, much to the chagrin of Mom and Dad.

A rule that is also pretty standard of everywhere you go is if you get a funny bounce that lets the ball stay on the table and roll back to you. If this situations comes into play you may throw a behind the back toss towards your opponent's cups. This is a low percentage bonus considering I only see about 2% of these shots go in. Another low percentage occurrence is if you throw the ball and it goes in your opponent's cup they are drinking out of. In this case, the game is either over or you have to take away another cup. The majority of places I have played tend to lean towards the removal of a cup only.

BONUS TIP: When picking your partner you can take two approaches. If you are trying to talk it up with a girl it is a good chance to get her to come spend a decent amount of time with you in a competitive environment. This is often bonding and can lead to a drunken conversation later. On the other hand, it is wise to seek out a friend who is neither wasted nor completely sober to play with. It is good to find them in the buzzed state because they're just drunk enough that they can focus and stay steady, but not too drunk that their vision and balance is off.

Game 2: Flip Cup

Flip-cup is an incredibly simple game that gets a high degree of competition involved and a lot of people involved in the game. You line up with teams as little as 4 on 4 (four on each side of a table facing one another) and as many as the greatest number of people the table or counter will hold. The largest game I was involved in was an 11-on-11 match up at a friend's house party. But the game is a great deal of fun, perhaps because it's my best game. It is fast paced game with a pretty good edge on it.

The teams need to be even and there has to be multiple pitchers of beer or everyone having their own beer to keep re-filling their cup. Everyone needs a plastic cup and to fill it up about an inch high and set it in front of them at the table. Someone on the team will start the game across from them by first lowering their bottom of cup so it hits the table, then up to cheers the opponent across from them, then back down to lower the cup to hit the table, and then finally drink the contents.

When someone finishes their drink they immediately have to put the cup on the ledge of the table or counter and try to flip it a complete rotation so it lands upside-down on the table. Speed is the name of the game in flip cup. Once someone completes this task, their opponent to their right repeats the action without waiting for the other team. Once all team members finish the task, the round is over and a winner is named. It is a very simple game and you get drunk.

An approach I like to take is to line up not only across from someone I know so I can trash talk the whole game, but also beside some cute girl I want to talk to. The competitive edge is an icebreaker in itself so you really don't need to come up with something clever or excuse for talk to her. You will naturally converse with her throughout the game, and also have a friend across the table to get involved and make you look cool. If you're smart it will be a wingman across the table making you look good.

Game 3: Kings

This is a simple card game that involves a table full of people with the entire deck of cards spread out and facing downwards, surrounding a cup. The game does not require a great deal of attention and different rules will be applied attached to each card wherever you go. You keep playing this game until all the cards are gone, and then a new game will start back up. Players can come and go mid-game, which makes it a nice party favorite. These are the terms attached to the cards I most often see, and will forward to you. But you will find various rules all over the Internet that gives different meaning to cards.

2-You (Point at someone else to take a drink)

3-Me (You take a drink)

4-Floor (Last person to point to the floor has to drink)

5-Guys (All guys drinks at the table)

6-Chicks (All girls drink)

7-Heaven (Last person to point to the sky drinks)

8-Never Have I Ever (Everyone puts up three fingers and people go around the table saying something that they have never done starting with the dealer. If someone has done something the speaker hasn't they put a finger down. The first one to have all their fingers down drinks.)

9-Rhyme (The dealer of the card starts with a word such as "Car" that the person to their right has to rhyme by saying something like "Bar" for example. When someone can't come up with a word, they are the one who has to drink. A good weapon to pull out is the word orange if you're trying to get the next person drunk.)

10-Category (You bring up a category such as "Car Companies", "Shoe brands", "Candy Bars", etc. and people have to come up with answers until someone is left blank or they repeat.)

Jack-Rule (A rule is brought up by a the person who pulls the card that is applied until the end of the game. If it is broken the person who breaks it has to drink.)

Queen-Questions (This is where if you pull the card you ask a question to someone at the table and they look at someone else and ask them a question, and so on and on until someone can't think of anything and they drink.)

King-Cup (At the beginning of the game the cards are surrounded around the cup. When someone pulls a king they pour a sizable amount of their drink into the center cup regardless of what they're drinking. This goes on for the first three people to pull kings, who all contribute a portion of their drink until the middle cup is at least half full. When the fourth king is pulled the person who pulled the card must drink the contents of the cup in the middle. It may be a combination of beer, mixed drinks, or some fruity drinks.)

Ace-Waterfall (This is where everyone drinks started by the person who pulls the card and as soon as they start drinking the person to their right has to drink and this continues the whole way around the table to include all players. When the person who pulled the card, or dealer, puts down their drink the person to the right can follow suit or continue to drink. But you can't stop drinking until you're either out of drink or the person to your right puts their cup down.)

Game 4: Up the River, Down the River (aka F*ck the Dealer)

This is the other of the two supreme drinking card games. It is probably even easier than "Kings" because it simply places the deck in the dealer's hand that put a card down facing the guesser. For example, he throws down a 7, the guesser then has to say higher or lower. If he/she is right when the next card is overturned than the dealer drinks, if not then the guesser drinks. This goes on until the dealer wins three times in a row, and then he passes the deck onto the next person.

The name gets the name of "F*ck the dealer" because as the deck starts coming out the dealer must arrange all the cards in order so everyone can see what was already handed out to make an educated guess. As the deck gets lower the guessing becomes more accurate, and the dealer drinks more and can't pass the cards on. But there is also an extreme version of this that asks for the guesser to be able to guess the exact card.

In this case the guesser throws out an initial guess on what they believe the card to be, and if they're right the dealer drinks but if not they get one more guess what the next card will be. If they are wrong the guesser drinks, if they are right the dealer drinks. This goes on until the dealer stumps three players in a row. This version is used to pass the deck faster around the group.

Game 5: Shark Week on Discovery

This game has a short description. You sit around for the one week a year and you have to take a drink from your mixed drink or beer every time you see a shark. The game lasts roughly 10-12 minutes before someone bows out because of the sheer ridiculousness. The game is enjoyable, gets you drunk, and is educational for all who are involved.

Game 6: Quarters

Quarters is probably the most classic drinking game in the history of drinking or games. You simply take a glass or a shot glass and try to bounce a quarter into the glass. You play in teams and the first team to get to a given number of quarters to go into the glass win the game. The losing team then has to drink the communal beer. This is usually only maybe a beer per person, so you're not sitting around collecting dust as someone painfully powers through cheap beer. Beer fills you up fast so you can only chug so much before you're looking for a shoe, hat, or potted plant to throw up in.

For the drunks: Power Hour

Really a power hour is just a fast way of pre-gaming before going out so you can keep a good buzz going for a while, but really it can be an entire night. I've had a couple nights end at the power hour and a couple of 40-ounce empty beer bottles at my feet. The power hour is dangerous so I recommend picking a wise drink seeing that every 60 seconds you'll be pouring some down your throat.

I highly recommend beer, because it is a standard drink and no one will make fun of you ever for drinking beer. But you can't be rolling up to an apartment as a man with any girly drinks like Smirnoff Ice or Mike's Hard Lemonade and not expect a few jokes and laughs at your expense. I'm sure you'll look real cute after you're drunk from a drink most middle-aged women drink on vacations to the beach. You can easily be judged by the type of alcohol you bring to an event.

Be safe and pickup some mid-range beer like a Miller Lite or Bud Light to start off the night. Regular Budweiser is OK, but you may fatigue before the end of the 60 minutes because it sits heavy. But you look like an ass if you quit before the end of the 60 minutes, so do not be soft and purchase cheap beer for this venture. You won't want cheap beer because it is the first thing you will drink that night, and that garbage tastes like tap water and you'll look like a cheap idiot in front of the ladies.

All right, finally onto power hours themselves. You can either do a video power hour, which is certainly more challenging than the audio power hour. I have run into various power hour mix tapes in my day from hits from the 1980s, sports highlights, television theme songs, techno, rap, nature sound effects, and many more. You should be able to put one of these mixes together and really get the early night hours hopping. An excellent program I used is Audacity, which as of this publication is free online. I believe the safe bet is making a tape out of classic rock hits, because as people get drunker they start singing along. You may be even able to sneak "Don't Stop Believing" and "Living on a Prayer" on the tape multiple times assuming the liquids are flowing, as they should be.

These two tunes are probably the most heard songs in a college town after 2:30 AM. I know this because I live downtown for four years in a college town and invariably, eight people are left in a living room somewhere with the sliding glass door open drunkenly singing along. It puts a smile on my face until some dumb girl gets out of line and either is out of tune or changes the song so she can "dance." She is usually wasted and left dancing to the beat of her own inebriated drum. I really do not know anyone who hates classic rock. If they don't, then they're probably a communist.

Make sure you have at least 4-6 people for a power hour so no one can just sneak away for 10 minutes and collect themselves. Once someone quits they are out of the race, the only break is for bathroom break. No cell phones, Facebook, texting, or anything of that technological garbage stuff to delay the game and take a player out of action.

BONUS ACTIVITIES:

Here are some bonus activities I have picked up throughout my five years of college that can really spice up a party. The first game I learned as a young sophomore was called Suck-Blow; apparently a game known nationally. Essentially, you have about 8-10 people around a table arranged in girl-boy-girl-boy-girl-etc. and you have to pass on a playing card from person to person using nothing but your lips. Obviously, much like a kiss you suck when the card is being passed onto you and blow when you are doing the passing. If the card is dropped, then the two people who break the pass have to take a drink. It is a fast-paced game that will most likely get you drunk, a girl, and later on a cold. But it is worth it.

A game I learned while playing Ultimate Frisbee my fifth year of college was called drinking a disc. This is a game usually reserved for Ultimate Frisbee players only, but for the sake of fun I will pass it on. You fill up a disc with beer, which holds a mind-boggling 4 and 1/2 beers, and the participants lay flat on their stomach face down in the disc. When told to go, the participant must continuously drink the beer from the disc without using their hands.

If you stop, you get a 10 stall count, just like the time allowed a Frisbee player to throw the disc without turning it over; very much like a shot clock in basketball. If one of the officials of the race notices you haven't drank in 10 seconds they can keep pouring beer into the disc until the participant starts drinking again. The race is only over when all beer is consumed. I throw out this caution; you can't have a weak stomach because trashcans are mandatory for vomiting.

Lastly, an activity more so than a game is completing what is known as the beer triple-crown. You need to shot gun a beer (poking a hole in the side then popping the can open so it funnels out into your mouth), keg-stand (have some friends help you out for safety purposes as you drink straight from the keg tap), and lastly the beer bong. I would not recommend doing any of them within five minutes of one another unless you are clinically insane, but it will make for an interesting night. I have completed the triple-crown a number of times in my college career at parties; the key is not throwing up and making a fool and mess of yourself.

Robo-pound is a game that came across my way as a sophomore at Penn State-Altoona. It involves a team of two players on each side. Each group has six cups and there is one large cup in the middle holding a full beer that the loser will eventually drink. Each team is given a quarter and each of the six cups for both are full of about an inch to two inches of beer.

When someone says go, the players alternate bouncing the quarter off the table and into the cup. The other team does the same until someone makes a cup, and the cup is then passed across the table for the other team to drink while they have to forfeit their quarter to the team who just sank their quarter. Whenever the beer is gone, the quarter is taken out of the cup and the team who was given the beer with the quarter in it can start bouncing the quarter to try to get it in cups. The team who sank the quarter in the cup and gave it up can continue bouncing as soon as they get the forfeited quarter.

This process continues until one team has sunk a quarter in all six cups and passed them over to the other team in exchange for their quarter. Lastly, the giant cup with a full beer in it that rests in the middle of the table is attacked by the team after they finish off sinking all six of the cups that were originally on their side. Once one team sinks their quarter in the center cup, the game is over and the losing team has to consume the center beer as well as whatever cups they were unable to sink quarters in on their own side. The game is then over, and the cups are refilled. It is a fast-paced fun game that usually has lots of yelling and cheering.

I will address spring break trips, because it is one giant party that never ends. It is essentially you getting drunk on the beach; recover, only to start the process again later that night before the club. You better load up quickly, not have any glass bottles, get out and enjoy the fun in the sun because you only have so many spring break trips in your system. There is really nothing bad about the trip at all once you get there, except if a friend gets arrested for stealing bread sticks from a Pizza Hut then placed in the back of a cop car.

Girls from all over the country, sun, beer, and the beach; what else could be better? Not a whole lot in the world can top these great times to be had at spring break. It is a mid-semester trip to get away from the grind of projects, sub-freezing temperatures, and the same old routine. You need to go on spring break at least once throughout your college career, even if you don't drink. It is a crazy and a relaxing time all at the same time.

This will probably be the most important trip of your college career. If you are lucky you will be able to go on spring break multiple times to enjoy a week of relaxing and drinking, most likely by a pool or beach. The media makes spring break look a lot crazier than it is, but it only gets as crazy as you make it. But not everything that happens on spring break stays there; it usually comes back as a STD or a YouTube video. Have a great time, but don't be an idiot.

First rule of spring break is that you plan it with a small group, at most four or five; after that there are too many opinions coming into play and too much money to collect. There will always be someone who says they are good to go, but then backs out so you can't go screwing yourself. When someone falls, you need to rally the troops and hope they don't fall like dominoes. If you're hearing opinions from six, seven, or more people you will need to split into two groups.

If you're going to go on spring break go all out on a nice place. Don't be the jackass who goes to Virginia Beach for spring break when you go to the University of Virginia; expand your view more, a lot more. There should at least be one day consumed going to and from your destination either through driving or through the air. We drove from State College, PA to within an hour of Panama City Beach in one day on our way down, or about 20 hours. We actually made it back in one day over about 20 hours at the end of the week.

I actually got in at my apartment at 5:30 AM and was supposed to be at work at 10 AM. I put my stuff on my bed to lay down for a minute, the next thing I know I wake up and it is 4:15 in the evening. I had literally slept through an entire day of work, something that baffles me to this day. But that was how much time and energy we had devoted into making the trip, and you need to leave everything on the table for this trip.

Spring break is the trip that you will be talking about 75 years when you're a babbling old man in a nursing home somewhere. It is a terrific time as long as you're open to all kinds of new things you will encounter. When my friends and I made the trip we played a great deal of sand volleyball and came across drinking games we've never seen before. One such game was dizzy bat, which soon became a favorite that traveled back with us to Pennsylvania. You essentially fill a waffle bat full of beer and chug it, while the crowd counts. However many seconds it took you to drink the beer is how many spins you do before stepping up to the plate and hitting your smashed can with the bat.

If at all possible, get a room that has a mini-kitchen in it to cook in. Then you can go grocery shopping and stock the fridge full of food and drinks for the enjoyment of the trip. If you have the kitchen you don't have to waste time going out to get food, you can relax in the room while it cooks. It probably won't be overly nutritious or well thought out, but the food will counteract the booze you consume all day on the beach.

Just deny getting your room serviced the entire time you stay at the beach because there will be all kinds of clothes, sand, and crap all over the room. We had two girls' numbers on our mirrors throughout the length of our stay in Panama City Beach. It was written in deodorant and was incredibly awful coming off whenever we had to leave and get our deposit back. We got the entire deposit back except $15, from a chair that was stolen from our balcony by some unknown freak of nature while we were gone one night. The beaches will be like one giant party about every ¼ mile as you walk, so makes it count.

Bars and Clubs

Once you turn 21 you will have the options of adding bars to your list of possible social destinations. Most clubs will have an 18 and over night sometime during the week; but once you turn 21 the club has a significantly different meaning to it. You are now allowed to drink and keep the buzz going instead of drinking cheap Vodka right before entering the club. Now you're the old guy hitting on the 18 year old girls dancing on the floor.

Not all bars will be your types because it depends on the crowd and the prices. You have taverns, piano bars, underground bars, pubs, sports bars, alumni bars, college bars, holes in the wall, and a bunch of other types of places. You will need to find your style, but it is important to spread the wealth because of the various specials offered by bars throughout the week. This is the way to save money and intermingle with a variety of crowds that you may not meet if you stay at one place.

Educating yourself on etiquette and approach is absolutely essential to having a good time and saving money at the bar. Just like anything research will help, but experience is even better. The last thing you want to do at a busy bar is get there, have the bartender's attention and not know what you want. The bartender has probably 15 people waiting for her and has very little patience for you. Know where you're going and what you want when you get there so there is no dead time.

Most towns will have a site that lists the bars, entertainment and specials that night. Make sure you refer to this if you don't know the area very well or are new. Most of your friends your age will have no idea what place is best, and the last thing you want to do is drop $5 cover on a place that is empty and there are no specials. Then you're locked into that decision, because after about a month of the school year $5 is a lot of money to be throwing away.

An important thing to know before going out is that there are certain drinks that you need to avoid to dodge humiliation. The last thing you need is being made fun of for having a red ring around your mouth from some stupid girly drink you voluntarily had at the bar. Your friends are going to ask you if you blew the Kool-Aid man; not funny nor cool. They won't let you forget it for at least a month because it'll show up in four or five Facebook photos.

Nothing with artificial fruit juice should be involved with any of your drinks or fruits outside of the lemon or the lime in any of your drinks. Outside of these citrus fruits, the next closest thing you should come across is a worm in the bottle. Speaking of which stay away from margaritas, because your girlfriend across town will be drinking them with her friends watching some stupid movie like 13 Going on 30. You don't want to have the awkward conversation later that you both were drinking margaritas on the same night because she'll make you drink them all the time. This will lose you serious dude points with your friends.

You won't hear the end of it if you walk into a get together drinking a Hard Lemonade, Smirnoff Ice, wine cooler, or any sort of Daiquiri or Martini. You will be called Ma'dam all night, chairs will be pulled out for you, doors opened for you, and odds are you will be offered wine. Wine is all right, but only if it bought with the intention of drinking it at a high rate of speed. You have plenty of time to drink wine when you're 40 years old by your fire place, so don't sit there smelling the cork and gargling it like you're an expert. Also don't drink champagne unless its New Year's Eve, you're at a wedding or you just won a world championship in a major sport.

For starters, no one will ever make fun of you for having a beer in your hand because there is nothing more laid back and masculine than having an ice cold tall long neck brew in your hands. Women will just think you're a regular guy out enjoying the night with your buddies if you've got a beer. You don't need to be a jerk ordering some random beer that is not on the specials list, because only idiots don't drink the house special. You may say, "Well, that's what I like," and then I would say, "Well, you're a tool for spending $18 on three beers because I'm drinking $2 pitchers."

Drinking mixed drinks is acceptable; but if you're a gamer you will take shots and wash them down with a beer. This isn't always a good thing because some guys do not know when enough is enough and keep taking shots thus making it a short night. You're not a cowboy so it really isn't necessary to take more than a few shots. If not, you end up having to carry them back to your building, because they decided it was a good idea to take a shot for every touchdown in Madden they scored on rookie level.

For more elaboration on drinks, I bring back Christen and Brittany to comment on what they think about a guy with general drinks. I've given you the perspective of one man viewing another man with types of drinks. But the type of drink you order can also make a difference in how you're viewed by girls:

Beer

Christen: All-american guy! If it's something like Miller Lite or Bud Light, he's obviously buying it to get drunk, not for the taste. Yeungling or Blue Moon, he actually cares what he drinks. Bottles over drafts.

Brittany: I like when a guy has a bottle rather than a draft. And uses his pointer and thumb to hold it, and tips it back with his middle finger. He seems more relaxed with a bottle.

Mixed drinks i.e. cranberry & vodka, captain & coke

Christen: It's a little girly, but it's the route I take, so I'm not hatin'.

Brittany: He's trying to get drunk or it's on special

Shots:

Christen: If a guy buys you a shot, he's trying to go the extra mile, whether it be to get in your pants, or really impress you...because after the shot, chances are they're buying you a drink! (this is totally different if they're friends)

Brittany: If it's tequila he's my man!

Now that we have addressed the type of drinks that are acceptable to my friends, it is time to move on to the pre-game. Pre-game before going out because it will give you a quieter environment to talk to friends and girls before going to bar or club. It will also save you tons of money, and not make you binge drink nearly as much by trying to squeeze all your drinking into a two-hour period to save money before specials end. It is also a time when you can show off various drinks and games you've learned to friends to have some fun before heading out.

There will always be some sort of argument on where everyone wants to go, probably because there will be two specials running simultaneously. This will provide a problem for the group as a whole because it wastes valuable time that could cost the momentum of the night. It's always worthwhile to take a quick vote, and if someone wants to break off, that's fine. It's no big deal you should be worried about, and people surprisingly turn it into a bigger deal than they should. That is why it impossible to travel in a group any larger than about six people and have common destinations.

Before you even get in you have to go through the bouncers who think they are working at an embassy or something. They check your ID, back-up ID, and then they test the durability of both cards by looking at the holograms, date of birth, testing the plastic, looking at the scan line on the back, and anything else they can think of before charging you $5 and your girlfriend $2. Face it, as a college guy you will continue to get screwed paying more and being invited less places. The sooner you accept it, the better the time you will have.

A college bar is no place to make a statement by ignoring the specials, because the specials are why 90% of the people are even there. It's not because of the atmosphere, because if it were 25 cent draft night out at a utility shed kids would show up to it. So at least when you wake up hung over and look for the money in your pockets to go buy a Whopper you will be pleasantly surprised. You only spent $12 instead of being the jerk that drops $50 on non-special drinks.

The problem with specials is bartenders don't always clearly tell you what they are. Sometimes you get a real snake in the grass that will actually make the drinks you ask for without checking to see if you're sure because it is an unusual order. Next thing you know you have two drinks that cost you $10 each, like you're drug lord making it rain in the club. You will be supremely ticked off by the whole situation and it may even ruin your night because it digs far deeper into your pocket than expected. But you'll need to roll with the punches and rally.

Meeting women in bars or clubs is an awful way to approach the situation. In my experience, you have to go through friends to have any credibility of possibly being a nice guy. Friends are that bridge the girl needs so she knows she can check up on you after you meet up, but if you're some random Joe then you have nothing to stand on. From our perspective as guys, a girl could come down from a spaceship or walk off a Greyhound at that instance and be liked by us. Not the same with women feelings on men. Unless he looks like a tool, then for some reason girls love those guys. To them the guy has confidence to pop his collar and wear sunglasses in the club at 11 PM; but to us guys he is a fool.

Other men have made girls timid to meet new guys. Random tools that go up behind girls in the club or at the bar and try to dance with them. No one likes these honeybees of the floor going around from delicate flower to delicate flower trying to get some pollen. Most of the time, guys like girls to dance up on them unless she just is flat out gross, but so many guys hit on girls that it gets old and ruins it for all of us.

Try getting to know the girl before going out and getting that close with her because you don't know if she has a boyfriend with a short fuse ready bash your head in. I feel a good 10-15 minute conversation must be had before making the move to the dance floor, even if it is drunken chat because that at least is a mutual move to the floor. The main focus of chatting it up should be done through mutual friends to girls you know or meet.

You need to at least be able to hold your own on the floor, so you don't want to be too awkward and stiff because the girl will think you don't know what you're doing. But conversely you can't be too aggressive, because the girl will just think you're clinically insane. You need to find a nice common ground and let her lead the dance, because honestly she is the one who really came to dance. You just came to pick her up but don't let her know that.

As I've mentioned trying to avoid the girls night outs because they are like a mirage in the desert. It looks like something that is a layup, but turns out to be something it isn't. Then they look at you like you're an idiot because you didn't grab the program on the way in listing them as a no guys allowed group. Don't worry men will get trapped in these black widows' webs the rest of your life; you're not the only clueless one.

But it is important to get on the floor by midnight if you plan on going down. I have found that sometime around midnight at most bars I've been to a large influx of guys show up to try to pick up drunk girls. They are for the most part creeps who just clog up the dance floor and swallow up any wasted girls that stray away from their groups. It is an injured gazelle being attacked by a bunch of bloodthirsty lions, except if the lions were a bunch of dirt bag guys.

Make sure you keep an eye on your cell phone time or your watch all night so you don't order a drink out of happy hour time and screw yourself out of more money than you were expecting. The bar will always leave a couple of hours for people who are too drunk to comprehend what they're doing to order drinks. They will keep ordering crap that they think is on special and before they know it they've blown $30 that they don't remember the next day or when they get their credit card bill.

When tipping for drinks there are a couple of route you can take. In my experience, if I know it will be a busy night at the bar I will tip the bartender up front and tell them to keep coming back to me. I will usually tip them $5, which is a pretty decent amount to get from one person in a night and especially in one dose. This usually works and you will get your drinks quickly and there is not much time of standing there feeling ignored. It only works if you get there before it gets busy though, so take that as a word of caution.

The other approach is paying after each round, which is better if you will only make a couple of trips and don't plan to be at the bar long. But try to get a few drinks under the same trip because you'll save money on tipping. Bartenders won't be happy but they're pulling a dollar or so from about half the people they're making drinks for. They have to be pulling $30-$40 an hour depending on how busy it is. So that is about what I made in a day working part-time so I would never complain.

Don't do anything dumb that gets you kicked out of bars like getting in a fight with some jerk or stumbling everywhere. I've had a good number of friends kicked out of bars before for slipping on water coming out of the bathroom, breaking an ashtray, hitting a hot air hand dryer, shoving matches, falling asleep, and falling down stairs while wearing a giant foam sombrero. These are normal occurrences in a college town and the bars that facilitate to the school's student body. Now enjoy!

Recovering from a Hangover

Tip from a bartender: "Get up at 7 AM, chug a Gatorade then go back to sleep."

Battling a hangover is usually a work in progress for most college students because no one tells them the proper way to go about attacking these triumphant roadblocks to productivity. Usually the worse the hangover, the better the previous night was and lower quality of the alcohol, but that is just wishful thinking. The proper way to deal with a hangover is to attack it before the drinking the night before even begins. This means foods and drinks that will be able to slay this dragon of a beastly headache you will have the next day.

It may be easier to solve a Rubik's cube than it is to avoid a hangover after a great night out on the town. But if you do not want to be a waste for two-thirds of the next day, follow my instructions to beating the odds. The process begins with your trip to the liquor store and selecting appropriate liquors to make yourself look classy, avoid sickness, and get at an affordable price. The rule is do not buy anything in a plastic bottle if you do not want to projectile vomit or feel like you got hit by a car the next day.

The only time it is appropriate to buy plastic bottled liquor is when you will not be the one drinking it. It should only be used to mix into a jungle juice from or to clean toilets, because these liquors are only appropriate for hobos and cheap frat guys. But when you look at the top shelf of liquor to only reason to purchase it is if you plan on going to a meet and greet with Snoop or Kanye. Patron and Grey Goose are not really necessary and their products are not that much better than the middle of the road liquors. You will look like you are trying too hard.

When you buy these types of alcohols, it usually only means you're a stereotype and easily swayed. You heard them mentioned in a rap song, and you figured you'd be on the in by dropping $50 of your $160 check you just got for selling your books back on booze. People who are real veterans of drinking know what they like and very rarely jump around from brand to brand. It took me about a year to settle on my favorites of Southern Comfort and Sailor Jerry's. All middle shelf bottles of liquor that will neither break the bank nor make me look like someone that has no idea what he is doing.

I tend to stay in the middle shelves of the liquor store because no one will call you cheap, but you're not trying to show off as I said. When you are at your place and people see you, they will think you are just set in your ways and that is what you like. That will make you look distinguished, and will save money while battling the potential hangover. I recommend starting the night with clear liquors such as some gins and all vodkas, because for whatever reason they are less rough on your stomach than brown liquors. But it is nice to have a balance of both brown and clear liquors present in your collection because your mood will change night to night.

If at all possible, try to stay with one type of liquor throughout the night. At most, you want 2-3 but when you start jumping around an angry fight will begin in your stomach. No, it wasn't the chilly fries or the milkshake you had, although those won't help, it is the cornucopia of spirits you have in your gut not getting along. Next thing you know it'll be four hours later and you won't be sure why you're covered in Sharpie or grass stains. Everyone will laugh at you as you walk home at 6 AM without a jacket and with many renderings of male genitals covering your exposed skin.

Before you even start drinking make sure you eat a meal of substance, preferably involving bread products of some kind. A couple of McDonald's Big Macs is a bad example though because you will probably end up getting the Texas Two Step at some point throughout the night. I suggest a nice couple of slices of Sicilian pizza or an Italian bread style of the turkey sandwich, anything that will involve lots of bread to soak up booze. You need to create a buffer between liver abuse and your booze; plenty of bread will do just that.

To accompany this bread full meal, get a drink that will keep you re-hydrated such as water, Gatorade, or Vitamin Water. You have to stay away from beer, pop, energy drinks, or anything that will make the hangover worse. All the liquor and beer you will be taking in will do all the dehydration for you as you are out on the town. So now you have a good 20 ounces of water in you and a solid bread based meal in your stomach, you're ready to go. If at all possible, get mixed drinks that have fruit juice in them such as cranberry and vodkas or screwdrivers.

We've already discussed what you should be picking out to drink to look classy and not feel like one of the extras killed in the movie 300 the next morning. At the bar, make sure they are giving you decent brands of liquor in your drinks, because if you ask for a cranberry and vodka they will give you the ever so dangerous hose vodka. This vodka is usually a plastic bottle brand that is bought in mass quantities from the bar and stored in a tank. By itself it tastes like pure concentrated Russian cat piss, so ask for name brands if you can. You put in all this effort to avoid crappy low-shelf alcohol, why give into it when you can have higher priced liquor at the same cost on well drink night?

The phrase "Beer before liquor, never been sicker" and "Liquor before beer and you're in the clear" is somewhat true. You can chase shots with beer and we regularly did it at the bar if someone bought me one. But other than chasing a shot it is a bad idea to drink a beer, then take three shots and go back to beer. We can reference the chemistry class example I provided a couple paragraphs ago. Whenever the night is winding down or you want to take it easy you should turn to beer because no one will call you soft if you're holding a beer. Try your very best not to go back to liquor to lower the percentage of vomit in the forecast after making the switch to beer.

Eventually you'll get the alcohol munchies and this is the time to have another medium-sized meal with a hydrating drink. For this specific meal your options for drinks is expanded from just water to allow the use of Gatorade and Powerade products that contain electrolytes. The problem with drinking these before going out on the town is you still have not been dehydrated and still have electrolytes in your system. Going out you sweat and have drinks that go right through you that such fluid out of your system causing you to get drunk faster.

Replacing these electrolytes while corresponding with a meal will put the necessary elements back into your system to soak up alcohol that is still in your stomach, replace lost electrolytes, and rehydrate the body of fluids. Most people forget to have this meal and pass out instead; but will surely wake up in a few hours with the spins and a headache. Have a glass of water next to your bed just in case you do not have enough fluids in you and you wake up feeling overheated from dehydration and need to cool down.

The next day a popular option amongst most people is the greasy foods with a tall glass of water to wash it down. I'm a big fan of Five Guys, so that really hits the spot after a sick morning brought on by poor liquor or a poor approach, and ignoring my own advice I throw out in this book. There seems to be some infatuation with fatty foods the day after a heavy night of drinking, and my philosophy is you already feel like you have been hit by a truck, so how can a Big Mac possibly make you feel any worse than you are right now? This is a great question, because once you hit rock bottom you can't dig any deeper so you might as well pile it on. But once you get back in the gym, it's go time until the next outing.

You hopefully won't have anything important to do the day of a hangover. I remember one such story of me going out for my 21st birthday and killing three pitchers of Jack and Coke. This is before I wised up and realized that pop dehydrates you and obviously Jack Daniels is quite effective. Don't get me wrong it was a terrific night, but not highly recommended when you have important things to do the next day.

I woke up the next morning with the spins, but determined to get to my 9 AM class. After a 20-minute walk of recovery I got to class and was informed we were going to be watching a movie. I thought this is great to myself, the lights will be out and I'll be able to relax. Then I quickly found out that every shot was from a helicopter spanning a plot of land. By the end of the movie, my desk was covered in sweat that was rolling off of my chin. Awful decision, one I hope you can avoid.

That Guy: The Pursuit to Not Be Him

There is a very dubious honor handed down to a guy who seemingly acts in a way that is socially unacceptable. That distinctive award goes to men known as "that guy" at a party, bar, or any social setting that makes others uncomfortable. These guys are a cancer to the fun of any social event, and if you're not careful you can easily become that guy. It happens to the best of us, some naturally have that lack of charm, while others simply have bad luck in a situation.

The Crop Duster

For clarification sake here are some terms my buddies and I used for stages of the craps:

- **Bubble Guts**-The first instance of you feeling gas and the impeding danger of potential pooping your pants.

- **Texas Two-Step**-This is the speed walk you do to the bathroom that usually involves extreme stops to let bubble gut explosions in the intestines to pass and let you continue your journey.

- **Ragin' Cajuns**-This is the end result once you get to the toilet. No more explanation needed.

What is important to know about parties and bars is that there is not an option to go take a #2 in many locations. There are people at the party and bar waiting in line for the bathroom who will judge you when you walk out of the bathroom and you've left the entire hallway to kitchen section of the party unbearable. Needless to say, your buddies won't jump up to defend you or the tuna salad you had earlier in the night. Eat healthy and smart before going out on a drinking session. Bread the evening before and greasy food the next day to counteract the effect of alcohol.

If you are faced with a potential case of the Ragin' Cajuns in a social setting make sure to know your surroundings because you will need to move fast, but not too fast, to the facilities. You will probably be standing out talking to a girl, by the keg, or at your table when the bubble guts make their presence known. The entrance of the bubble guts is when you know it was not a good idea to eat a cheese steak for dinner but that is not important. What is important is getting to the can as soon as possible. As soon as the bubble guts make their presence, the shot clock has been set.

The problem as stated is that taking a deuce at a party is not acceptable socially and I'm pretty sure legally. The problem at a bar is that the bathroom, if it even has stalls, will be horribly disgusting because of other guys coming in and letting it all fly like it's a blind guy at a shooting range. It is at that instance you finally understand female disgust with men not putting the toilet seat up. It certainly gave me a new appreciation for sure.

Before you go out on the town with the knowledge that the Ragin' Cajuns may come up later in the night, plan out some safe houses that you can frequent. These are places where it is OK for you to drop the kids off at the pool and it will be conflict free; ideally be within walking distance of your own home turf. The possibility of being close to your own bathroom, where maximum comfort occurs is not always possible however; so knowing a couple of late-night restaurants is key.

Cleanliness is not a top priority when you are on the shot clock created by the introduction of the bubble guts. The bubble guts automatically lead to the Texas Two-Step that is a combination of tight cheek speed walking combined with abrupt stops to let the worst pass so you can continue the journey to a safe house. But really only you will know how much time the bubble guts have left before the end result of the Ragin' Cajuns rear their ugly head. If a clean place is worth the little extra walk, go for it.

Getting there is half the battle; once you get to your destination you are usually a nervous wreck. Despite the fact these places you have listed as safe houses are OK; you still worry about outside pressure from other users of that facility. If you go to a restaurant, then it is only a matter of time before the impending doom of someone else knocking. Worse yet is a friend's place, most notably a girl friend's place. Those places are usually super clean when you go in, certainly much cleaner than your stinky joint. You need to minimize the damage as much as possible so you don't get the stink eye.

The advantage to going at a friend's place is you will probably be able to take your time and there will be reading material. There are some dangers that go with the friend bathroom drop-off option because you will leave a horrible stench, there is not nearly the interference noise that a restaurant has so you will be putting on a brown trumpet solo, and your friends will probably tells others about your ten minute "swung-by to say hi but was in the can the whole time" session. Regardless, of where you choose to go you will most likely be sweating like Rocky Balboa after the 11th round of a title fight when you get back to your friend's place a half hour later.

The Man Whore

You also do not want to be the guy who gets with every girl and her friends because gossip with girls spreads faster than a wildfire in a drought engulfed Southern California. Often, girls will make the statement that if a girl gets with a lot of guys she is considered a slut, but if a guy does it he is considered the man. This may be unfortunately true, but it depends on his judgment of the type of girls he is taking back with him. If he is getting the girls he sets out for at the beginning of the night, then yes he is the man; but if he is going for whatever he can get then he is a "man whore" much in the same way as girls who settle for whoever they can get are a slut. The door definitely swings both ways for both sexes, but it just depends on how they approach the night and the goals going in.

Going out looking for a Ms. Right Now is an approach taken by some I have known. This approach is certainly a bad one because girls always seem to have a link to one another at a college campus through mutual friends. Despite your thoughts that what you did was smooth; you check your Facebook account the next day to see a friend request from the girl you were trying to pick up the previous night. The problem is when you accept her request she has about 20 mutual friends with you and at least one of them is always some other girl you value more.

Like most men known as "That Guy," the "Man Whore" will travel alone, because he does not have many close friends just countless numbers of acquaintances that make him look like the man. Rarely, if ever, will you see him in a relaxed bar setting just enjoying the company of friends and the environment. Every day is spring break for this guy who believes that college should be his own personal "Girls Gone Wild" experience. He feels this way because he owns the entire director's cut version of every one of the films ever made so he can learn tips to use.

The problem is they will go through 10-15 girls before they land their winner. This girl will usually be one who is not horrible looking but is about 25 pounds too heavy and may smoke. They will certainly be no girl to write home to Mom about; usually just a conversation that starts with "I don't want to talk about it" the next day to a normal guy. But to Mr. Man Whore he will talk the girl up into you thinking she is the next top model.

The Right Angle Creep

This guy stands in the corner by himself or with another creep of the corner and checks out girls. He has a look of seriousness on his face like he is picking out a new car. What he is really doing is estimating drunkenness in girls throughout the party and calculating his odds as he stands in the corner away from everyone else. Occasionally, someone will come over by the keg with him and say a few words but this guy will not deter his attention and will mumble a few worthless time filling responses.

This guy thinks that college party life is a giant stakeout and he is a hotshot undercover cop who needs a big score. But he doesn't have the social skills or charm to straight up impress a girl through speech; he has to wait until she is completely drunk to swoop in and be Casanova. He probably will just be sipping beer even though he is standing right by the keg just so he knows he has the upper hand in sobriety when he finally does make his move.

Rarely there will be a second R.A.C. in attendance, but the two will usually know each other from a previous party or get together. They will have the most boring and vague conversation between them, but will compare notes for a second opinion on what girl is tipsy and who is simply bubbly. They will never play wingman for one another, just simply compare and contrast so that they can be surer there will be a certain degree of success.

The U.F.O.

This is the "Unidentified Freakin' Oddball" who just walks into an apartment party and no one knows. The problem is this guy is not even drunk, which can at least be somewhat condoned due to your drunken state. This guy will probably be a local product who never went to college but loves the social life and girls or he is just a guy who never left school. He is most likely at least 25 years old and travels the night solo going from apartment party to apartment party looking to find a girl he can make out with. But he is generally a nice guy even though he is odd as hell; so no one wants to confront him to tell him to leave or asks who he knows because everyone assumes there is a link somewhere.

The problem is that this guy doesn't know anyone at the party and is in the market to score some numbers of both guys and girls of the group. He will find some loose fitting interest with someone and immediately asks for their phone number so they can hang out later. This guy is like a cavity; as soon as he sees a weakness in the enamel he attacks the whole tooth. On a great night, this guy will leave with three or four numbers of people at the party, all of which he intends to call before you wake up so that you can have a "World of Warcraft" date or fly kites.

Most of your friends will ignore the call or the text message, but there will always be the person who has a conscience and invites this guy over again. That is when he really goes to work meeting people and taking note of names for him to go home with. After this guy latches on with the phone numbers and Facebook accounts he has won, he will be coming over periodically to hang out. He will never be a major presence in your group of friends, but one that you often question how the hell he got into the group years down the road.

Senor Overestimate

This guy anticipated the party to be far crazier than what it is when he shows up. That's why he took nine shots before leaving his dorm or apartment. He is not the type of guy who can hide his drunken state very well, and will probably be having problems with his balance as his body adjusts to the booze. He will awkwardly hit on girls who just started drinking and are not into his mumbling incoherent pick up lines yet. But he will try to escalate the drinking at the party by trying to make people do beer bongs and keg stands before they are ready.

This guy will keep the same pace as what he did before he left for the party and hope everyone else keeps up. But all the other people at the party realize that you just can't jump into pounding alcohol that quickly into the night. It is like running a sprint without stretching; something is bound to go wrong to ruin the entire night before it begins. Just as the party is getting going, the drunk guy will probably throw up somewhere in the apartment and he may or may not rally by getting a beer from the keg and hoping no one noticed. I walked into a party once with puke six feet up the wall from one of these guys.

Within a half hour this guy will probably pass out on the couch with his shoes on while there are still 50 people in attendance. Needless to say, Sharpies and markers will be brought out to turn this guy's skin into a real life canvas. He will wake up with a marker mustache, penises, swastikas, Dirty Sanchez's, and comments questioning his sexuality written all over him. He will awkwardly have to walk home extremely hung over to take a shower and get all the masterpieces off his skin before passing out into bed to sleep for 11 hours.

The Motivational Speaker

The motivational speaker usually is visiting from a different college or may be coming back to his old stomping grounds at age 27 and found his way into a pre-game drinking session. Nothing you will do is up to his standards or what he does at his school or in his day, but he assures you that you should have been there. You are absolutely certain that he was probably playing the same drinking games and consuming the same amount, and he is just embellishing his estimates.

No one outside of a couple people knows who this guy is or are listening to his rambling tales. But he will speak over everyone else and try to fire up the group to do things his way, because it will simply be more fun. Eventually, a few people might try his silly new drinking game, but will probably give up on it because of his poor explanation of how the game works. By the time it is time to leave, this guy will give up hope and will try to be talking it up with some girl to set himself up for later in the night.

Dennis Downer

Here's a guy who is always having a bad day and lets everyone know about it through Facebook status updates and near crying as he tells his woeful tale to whoever will listen. It is just your average day, but it is the end of the world for this guy. Despite you winning $100 in the lottery and landing a job, you have to hear about how this guy thinks he has an earache and how is always so tired. He looks on the bad side of every situation and can turn the happiest times into an involuntary heart-to-heart.

The worst part is girls that will dig him because he is so in touch with his emotions and how he is open to express them. This guy holds up the girls who make you sit around with your other guy friends for an extra 15-20 minutes listening to his week that sounds exactly like yours but in a depressive tone. You just want to go out on the town and leave on a good note to begin a wild and crazy adventure, but this guy constantly reminds you about his lack of success with women. He is a pretty good friend, but his dopey state usually is a burden as you look at him drinking by himself in a booth off the dance floor. But don't worry the booze will only fuel the depressive flames this kid has got burning. Don't be surprised if he cries by the end of the night.

The Undeniable Traits of a Tool

I've spent a great deal of time in bars/clubs in my five years of college. There aren't 15 minutes that goes by where my friends and I don't say, "Look at this tool." Now the problem with tools is that everyone probably has fouled up and broken one of the tool stipulations I've set forth. But for whatever reason we do what we do to get attention from girls. No longer is it enough to be a nice guy, but now you must make a statement and some of us get desperate for attention.

The problem is if you keep getting desperate and making drastic changes to the way you act and dress people will start pointing to you and saying "What a tool." We don't want this to happen, and that is why I set forth these common traits you find in many tools.

Here is a scale to see exactly how big of a tool you are:

0-2 Offenses-Saint

3-5 Offenses-Average to Fringe Tool

6-9 Offenses-There is a Line of People Who Want to Punch You in the Face

10+ Offenses-Better Go Into Protective Custody

The Traits:

Spiked Gelled-Hair

This is the hairstyle made famous by the Guido, as society has deemed to name him. But what was wrong with your hair before you made it flammable? Did you really need to spike it into one horn, like a unicorn? Having a little styling gel in your hair to give it shape is OK, bordering high maintenance, but acceptable. When it comes to you spiking your hair out like you just jammed a fork into a toaster, then you become a tool.

I Lift a Ton; so I can stare down anyone and everyone

These guys treat a trip to the gym like it's a Rocky movie staring down any guy they smell as weak. Don't worry about cardio or working on your legs because you're built like an upside triangle. The only place where you should be talking about how much you can bench is the NFL Combine and the gym, and neither is the club to a group of guys who didn't ask. We can probably tell that you lift just by looking; you don't need to break down your program to everyone.

Wearing Shirts that Have Reflective Material or Skulls

A tool will probably have a shirt that is light cotton that is probably too tight and occasionally comes up to show off the lower back and/or gut. Also does it need to be that tight? I mean you're not even jacked. There will probably be some stupid design like a dragon, flames, or something that looks like a 3-year-old's finger painting project transformed into aluminum foil design and placed on a cheap shirt.

These dirt bags will spend upwards of $50 on these shirts that apparently show they have some fashion sense. They also bought the shirt to make them look like they are ripped regardless if they are or not. It is like Under Armour gear for the club, with a stupid design. You will probably get mad when girls confuse this guy's lack of sense for confidence. He will have some decent girl hanging off his arm as he drinks a Washington Apple shot and talks about the car in the lot that he is leasing. He is only leasing the car during the school year to impress girls into thinking he is successful however.

Wearing a Sports Coat with a T-Shirt (aka the Don Johnson)

People have been rocking sports coats for a long time, and they're called NFL color commentators. This is a category you don't fit under. The only time you need to be rocking a sports coat is in the office or at the country club. $2 well-drink night at the Hooter's isn't exactly a fitting location for your t-shirt and sports coat look. Although I will laugh when you get wing sauce on your sports coat and need to take it to the dry cleaner.

Tan in February

Alright, now I can understand if you work outside in Miami but for the rest of us it's freezing. This can only mean one thing: you go tanning. But as a man, that is unnecessary because no man wants to be deemed beautiful by others. Usually if your buddies call you "Sweetheart," "Ma'dam," and "Douche," it usually isn't a sign of affection. Man up; be pasty and miserable like the rest of us.

The Man Nair Abuser

This guy spends hours in his bathroom with Nair, a personal trimmer, and many mirrors set up at various angles. Most likely he will be looking to sheer his fleece before he goes tanning and out to the club. It first starts with a fresh haircut, acceptable until they gel spike it. Secondly, comes the chinstrap beard that will surely follow. Then the craziness begins.

First goes the chest, belly, and back hair, which is acceptable but bordering the point of tool-like. Next comes the arm hair, which will get you metro comments from onlookers. Then go the armpits, which unless you're an Olympic swimmer is not welcoming to anyone. Lastly, on occasion the leg hair is shaved, so unless you're entering a celebrity drag show this is just weird. In parting, people like lumberjacks because they're real men not well manicured little ladies.

Ponytails

I don't even know what I could possibly tell you about ponytails that you don't already know. You're either a French art dealer, a pedophile, or are a Tai Chi Instructor. Anything outside of a religious haircut is completely unacceptable. Unless you're playing the part of a 1980's British villain for Halloween.

I'm in the military, which makes you a bad American

These guys are fighting for our country, which I greatly appreciate and respect, but they can be huge tools in the bar. Now I'm not saying it is all of them, or even really most military. But the guys who are the military tools really queue my buttons. They'll buy shots for the girls I'm with, but not me. This shuts down my momentum with the girls and looks to outbid me for their attention.

Be rest assured they will talk about their tours or ship-outs to try to impress the girl. This is an attempt to draw their affection and make you look like a bad American because you decided to go off to college and avoid the military altogether. Rest assured, this guy will end up hammered out of his mind and probably won't be a problem because of a poor alcohol tolerance. As you leave you notice he'll be dancing with a girl that outweighs him.

Finely Tuned Facial Hair

From the makers of the 30-minute shower comes the fine tuned facial hair guy. This guy will take the two hours it requires to make his chinstrap beard 1/16 of an inch just to show you how much he cares about his image. This guy spends more time in the bathroom than his girlfriend, which is a problem. These guys are typically delicate and highly selective in anything. He is definitely not a man's man that rolls with the punches.

Popped-Collar

Every now and then you press the issue in society and popping the collar of a polo shirt unnecessarily. Even more dreaded is the double collared shirt, which means twice the d-bag potential. Do any of these guys realize they look like Count Chocula selling cereal to all the kiddies? Yes, we understand you are wearing a polo shirt; you do not need to market the idea to the rest of us who wear ours correctly.

The "I'm Too Sophisticated For College Move"

These are the guys who will come out of nowhere to join your group drinking Manhattan's, Cosmo's, Gin and Tonics and other drinks Jack Palance and your grandpa would've enjoyed together. No one drinks these in college unless they are the 45-year-old Mom who came to visit her daughter and go out. Other than her and the professors, no one has the right to order these oldies in a college town.

The guy who carries these around tries to look sophisticated and set in his ways so women think he is classy. No, actually it provides the opposite impression, people think you go home and put on pajama pants, do the crossword, rub Ben-gay on your legs, then watch The Game Show Network. This isn't the kind image that you need to be putting off and if you're still confused order a beer. Beer is the Switzerland of drinks because no one judges you one way or the other based on a Bud Light or a Miller Lite in your hand.

The Paul Walker/Matthew McConaughey

If you have seen either of these gentlemen's films, you know they will use any excuse they can to take off their shirts. But you run into these jerks in everyday life as well. They will find any excuse to go shirtless and prance around showing off for girls. The problem is they usually aren't in great physical shape. Even with back hair, a small beer gut, and the beginning of man breasts this guy can make everyone uncomfortable at the smallest breeze of air. He'll ask who wants to see the "gun show," exclaiming those with weak hearts and small children should not view such a specimen.

If you're at a sporting event of any kind, off comes the shirt. When you're over at a friend's painting their new house, off comes the shirt. Whenever he smells a potential fight in the air, off comes the shirt. Anything over 55 degrees outside, off comes the shirt. Any manual labor that might produce sweat is started, off comes the shirt. If there is a basketball game this guy always yells for shirts vs. skins; then he takes off his shirt and says he is team captain. If he sees something that excites him, off comes the shirt and it is swung like a helicopter propeller over his head. In fact, the only thing he uses shirts for is cleaning his hands after getting them dirty.

Post-Drinking Donkey Kong

This is the guy who gets extremely emotional when he drinks and usually turns into physical aggression. They will instantaneously turn from a mild mannered sober guy to the Hulk punching and kicking holes into dry wall. They will run down the hall smashing beer bottles off of your door and kicking your door like they're Jason Statham in The Transporter during a revenge scene. When the night is said and done it will look like hurricane force winds went through their apartment.

Needless to say they will receive none of their apartment deposit back because of smashed glass and broken furniture all over the place when it comes time to hand in the keys. The problem is that these guys black out when they turn into the Hulk and do not take full responsibility for the damage they have done. For them, if they don't remember doing it then they probably didn't do it. They stay behind their stance that they did not punch out a window even though they have scabbed over knuckles, there were five eyewitnesses that watched him do it, and he brought pieces of the glass into his room with him.

He scares people when he gets drunk and there always has to be someone there to calm him down before he commits a serious crime. This is annoying because you always have to keep an eye on this kid while you're trying to have a good night. If he gets drunks early then you have to cut your night off early to take him home before he kicks in a cop squad car window. But he never remembers the next day to thank you.

The guy who overdresses for the bar he is going to be a wide margin

Whether it is a full suit or dress pants and suspenders this is unnecessary. We're at a sports bar or a college bar, no one dresses like they're a mafia wise guy. The sports coat wearer also goes hand-in-hand with the over dresser.

Busting Out a Guitar in a Social Setting

This guy will kill any momentum a party has by bringing out his acoustic guitar and telling everyone that he wants to play. He just started playing the guitar last year and wants to improve, but you know it is just to make himself look sensitive for girls. Everyone will have to gather round as he butchers "Free Fallin'" or "Hotel California" while girls admire his pursuit to learn the guitar. You and every other guy without musical talent can see right through his crap, but you can only communicate this to one another through body language and through a look in your eyes. Heaven forbid that you talk to one another or leave during this ultra awesome acoustic performance.

This guy needed something to push himself over the edge from being boring to the center of attention. The guitar was it, so he went to Wal-Mart and bought one for $129.87 off of the clearance rack and the punishment to the ears of his roommates began. The part that killed them wasn't the poor playing but the fact that he will only play Maroon 5, Jack Johnson and Dave Matthews songs because he knows girls are a sucker for their stuff. In fact, you like these artists too but this jack hole is really threatening your great play list.

The worst-case scenario is if another guy happens to have another guitar close by and it turns into a full-fledged douche jam session. The game is over for all the rest of the guys in the room because you know this garbage is going to go on for at least a couple hours. You're trapped but if you leave you'll look like a heartless monster. But you do the smart thing and abandon ship for your nearest watering hole to wait out the storm with your true friends who felt mutually about the situation.

Mr. CEO

This guy is always telling you about his future prospects and all the networking he is doing. He will always be on his cell phone checking e-mail, talking to a friend, or texting. Regardless of what he is doing he will politely nod and pretend to pay attention to what you're saying, but if he deems his cell phone task to be very important he will give you the all important "shush, just one moment" finger to the face that all of us hate. Are we in 2nd grade and need to be told when to be quiet?

He will rack up four full days a month spent on his cell phone, more time than you spend on yours in an entire year. He will also have roughly 4,000 text messages; if strung together could constitute a volume of a book series full of "LOL's," "what u up 2," and random other poor grammatical statements. Without his cell phone, this guy is Superman without his cape.

This guy may even be one of those jerks who always have the Bluetooth phone in his ear so you can't even visibly see that he is talking on the phone. He instead just looks like a lunatic who is talking to himself. The problem with this is you will be walking along and you pass him on the path while he looks ahead of you and smiles. He will say, "What's up?" and you stop to start talking to him, but he will just look annoyed and keep on walking. You can't tell under his shaggy hair or dread locks that he has a piece the size of a quarter sticking in his ear, and he is ticked off that you didn't have hawk-like vision to spot it.

This overachiever likes to boast about his accomplishments and consistently tells you about his resume. The problem is that you do not come from a rich area like this prick. Your parents were not part of some fancy country club making connections with other members to give a handout. You have had to work for everything that you have, and despite all that scratching and clawing you still end up behind this jackass going into the real world. Don't be this guy!

The One-Upper

This guy is not original at all; he will rely on you to come up with the subject and then tell a story that borders myth buster proportions that dwarfs yours. With every story this guy tells you will want to punch him in the face more and more. You graduated in four years, he was just short of graduating in three and a half; you made out with a girl, he took her home; you've been to London, he's been to Moscow; and so on until you have your fork tightly in your hand and want to jam it into his arm.

The worst part is the girl you are going after is buying his crappy stories that he is probably making up on the spot. She keeps saying things like "That's really interesting" or "Yeah, I'd like to do that," but only to his stories, which annoys you beyond belief. You can't call him out on a story unless he makes a major slip-up that you can question him on, but even if you do you will get dirty looks from the rest of the table who just adore this guy. The problem is he knows he is in competition with you and you can't question the legitimacy of his stories because he claims to have done something that you never have. Your only hope is that he gets caught up in his own lies and crashes and burns.

Other Guys You Will Probably Hate

This is one of the most obvious chapters because hardly a day passes when you don't see another human being that you don't hate before even meeting them. This differs from tool traits and being that guy. Because these are actual full-time identities. He could be the guy who obviously no longer cares about life because he's 50 pounds overweight and his crack is showing out of sweat pants or the girl who thinks she is too good to work at a grocery store. In college, image is a very important aspect of their life; but not that important. These guys probably just need drug out into the street and slapped because if you ever have to wait for a guy any longer than 20 minutes to get ready to go out, that is just far too long.

You will go to the bars or a party and just be angered at the sight of some guys. Most are guys you know you are smarter and funnier than, but yet they have a smoking hot girl on their arm and radiate of tool (see previous chapter). You will most likely have friends that are similar to you at such events who will be equally angered by the presence of the moron that just walked into the door.

A guy only needs so many male friends in their lives, while they can have countless numbers of girl friends. In fact, you will probably hate 75% of other guys you see at bars and parties. These are the guys you will be competing with for attention from girls and the respect of fellow guys. I think the important thought to remember is that nice guys tend to underestimate themselves because they have been humbled by past failures and go after only what they deem attainable girls. On the contrary, guys on this list of cupcakes tend to have all kinds of confidence and have a short-term memory towards women and getting shot down. In essence, they overestimate their self-worth by dressing like a rock star, but on a college student's budget because their image means everything. They will use dad's credit card to buy Patron and roll around in a BMW, but have no money to back it up like us modest less eccentric guys.

Below I have a list of types of guys you'll meet who you will instantaneously hate. They have multiple tool-like qualities, thus qualifying them as a douche bag. The problem is that a number of girls actually dig these stereotypical guys who just rip fashion tips from Kanye and pop culture. They have very little originality, and very little depth to their personality.

New Jersey's Finest (aka The Guido)

The Guido you'll probably be able to feel much like Darth Vader feeling Luke before seeing him. You will be able to spot these softies from a mile away with their gelled spiked hair, Kanye West style window shade sunglasses, mesh track jump suits, orange tan, and overbearing sense of entitlement. These guys literally think they live the life of a character on bad reality TV by driving nice cars and only talking to the greatest looking of girls.

They have sacrificed their worth to every other person in the club by ignoring their appearance which is borderline feminine because of all the waxing and shaving of body hair, most notably the chest and arms. These guys are nice stepping-stones for girls who used to be lesbians (so I am told) because they have many of the qualities of a girl because of their high maintenance to keep up with their looks. It is like riding a bike you need training wheels before you can coast into dating real men.

These guys also are the guys who will ignore all rules of fair play in a party. They will walk in and starting hitting on a girl you have been talking to for 45 minutes and look to start a fight with you all in a 90 second window. You will want to fight them, but the only problem in punching this "gangster" who learned all his moves from watching the Sopranos on his Digital HD television at his house in Jersey has a dad who is probably a high powered lawyer. He probably grew up in your dream house but yet he still claims he is from the streets and understands Snoop Dogg's pain.

Tall, Dark, and Handsome

This guy put in absolutely no work to give him the good looks that women adore, and you know it. He is the cousin of "The Lucky Bastard" below who you obviously hate because of his fortune for always having a girl in his lap. You have to walk 500 miles to get where this guy gets walking in the door. Patience is a virtue though because this guy's metabolism will eventually go to crap and he will gain 75 pounds, thus trapping the young foxy girl he used to hang with. She should have recognized the warning signs; especially when he sat around eating Doritos and playing Xbox instead of playing sports and working out.

The Lucky Bastard

This guy has no distinguishing factors that make him stand out from the rest of the guys at the bar. He was just born into the right situation, probably with a rich family that bought him a pretty nice car like a BMW or a Benz. He probably wears fairly nice name brand clothing that you can't touch with your $7.50/hour work-study job. He really isn't a good-looking guy nor that clever or smart; he simply just has all the connections.

This guy will be able to afford just about anything and will expect you to catch up. He does not consider the idea that you may not be receiving a trust fund because all his buddies from high school got one. It is just assumed that everyone gets $200/week from their parents like he does. He will always out dress, out drive, and out style you all while having a great looking girlfriend that uses him. He's just playing the waiting game until he is rich, set up by relatives.

He doesn't get great grades, but he has a hookup to a $75,000 a year job because his Dad plays golf with an executive for Exxon. You know he won't do a great job, certainly not as well as far more qualified people. But he probably has smoking hot girlfriend who is into him because he has money and always seems to get a tee time at the local golf course at peak times, while you have to wake up at 7 AM in a driving rainstorm. He probably has also won a TV or two in various giveaways or raffles on campus and doesn't even use them because he got a 54" flat screen from his parents for Christmas.

Wealthy Gangster

This kid has a father who is a doctor and a mother who is a college professor this kid will fill the need to act like he is from the hood, despite the fact that his parent's income is twice the size of your parents. Most likely this friend of yours will be black, but will get accused of acting white by other black people early in his college days. That was an awkward sentence coming from a white guy, but it is even worse to see in person. He is extremely smart and well-spoken, but for some reason he feels the need to act like the average hood gangster he sees in the media to gain acceptance from some of his own race. This is much to your surprise and disappointment, because of the state of society made him turn this way; but don't worry you'll see shades of the old him when he visits home for Christmas or calls home during the week.

Southern Frat Boy

These guys are weird because they dress different from anyone else their age. They look like my friend's 50-year-old father on a boating trip in the middle of July. Some sort of weird leather shoe that slips on without socks, short khaki shorts, with an Easter pastel colored Polo brand shirt tucked into the shorts, sun glasses that have the plastic version of the librarian strap, and to cap it off a visor. They will also have some sort of odd haircut you haven't seen since playing with Lego people that is short everywhere except where it counts right in front of the eyes. The hair will be bordering covering the eyes, but don't worry they will do a head jerk 14 times a minutes to keep it out.

These guys look like they could be ready to play in a poker tournament, go on a boating trip, coach an SEC football game, or play in a PGA tour event at any moment. They do not need to change attire because it is so ridiculous. The shorts look like they were stolen from Larry Bird's locker, the shoes from an 84 year old man in a retirement home, glasses from a guy in a Bassmasters fishing show, a visor from the Steve Spurrier collection, and a shirt that was taken from Dick from the Dick and Jane book series. Nowhere else will you find the spectacle that is these tools' attire.

These guys will be hammered drunk at the football game and dressed up. It will look like you are at a job fair and you'll be angry you did not bring your resume because maybe you would be able to score an internship with a visiting company. Actually they dress alike, and all look like bible salesmen.

Mr. Fabulous

These guys will be annoying to you as a straight guy. Certainly, what this guy does in his personal life is none of my business. But all the girls will love this kid because he is non-threatening to them because he won't hit on them and comments on other girls with them. It's like getting a hybrid perspective because he has the desires of women but the mind of a man.

He will probably at some point or another insult you for your lack of knowledge of pop culture, fashion, or your 5 o'clock shadow. Yes, you understand he isn't hitting on you because he knows you're straight. But you can't get mad at the kid and in fact you do not know how to react because your girl will most likely side with him because he is a close friend. Yes, you understand that you don't watch the Entertainment Network all the time, watch Project Runway, or take in American Idol but should that be held against you as a man? Probably not.

Looks like a Smut Film Star, but is just a Dirt Bag

This guy could either be a porn star or a sex offender. They are usually the ones you will find that have either a ponytail, some sort of large tribal tattoo, they're neither fat nor toned (kind of like Dog Bounty Hunter), never have a look of satisfaction, or have all of these qualities (qualities may be a poor word choice). No one really ever knows how old these guys are because they are usually tan at some unusual time of the year and they look like they never sleep. They usually are trying to hit on 18 year-old-girls when it is quite possible that they have fathered a girl who is already getting close to that age. They also work out in the gym and don't let you hear the end of it. However, they haven't done cardio since 1994.

These characters still believe they are living the greatest years of their lives even as they wake up with ulcers, a sore liver, and arthritis in their joints. They usually own a car that some girl may have appreciated 8 years ago, and can't afford a new one despite their job as a contracted painter. They typically wear jeans that are tight with a shirt tucked in to farther protect their gut and make the experience even that less enjoyable for everyone present.

The Silver Mustache

These are the guys who will always be alone coming into a college dance club and just sit at the bar. He could have picked any bar in the whole town including a good number that had a crowd around his age, but no he picked 18 and over night at the club. He claims he just came in to have a drink or two but he sticks around for three hours just watching, and will most certainly leave hammered drunk. You're not sure why he came to the bar; possibly the chance of a girl being hammered drunk and making one of the worst decisions of her life or simply he actually likes watching college girls. I mean who doesn't?

This guy randomly likes to come up and sit at your table and talk about things he did with girls in the 1970's. He completely throws you off your momentum you have working with the girl at the table across the walkway that you were hoping to capitalize on. Now you look like you're out with your drunk uncle, but you're afraid he will make a big scene and completely ruin your night if you tell him to leave.

This guy will joke around with the bartender who is usually a gorgeous girl who only got the job based on her appearance in a low-cut tank top. He will tip her well and think he has a legitimate chance with her at the end of the night. The only problem is he will instead have to call his brother or a friend at 2 AM that will wake up some kids so that this guy can make it home to go to bed. Needless to say he will be hung over at his job at Wal-Mart automotive at 2 PM the next afternoon.

The Pierre Frenchy

The random foreign guy, who is usually French or Australian, that comes in and talks to the girls you are with. Much like breast implants attracting men, the accent and goofy scarf on an 80-degree day takes the girls right from your arm. You better settle in too, because she will probably be talking to Harry Potter for a solid hour about motherland England. You couldn't care less, but you know this guy is only using his difference to try to score a number for a later meeting with your girl.

Your local accent is normal for the girls and far from exotic, so if she brings Hugh Jackman home to her girlfriends, they will fall in love with talking to the kid. The only problem is this character is there for a semester and will probably be looking to cause as much havoc as possible while he's in the states. Regardless, if the girl has a boyfriend or even if you're present, your girl will melt for Hugh Grant and his "sexy accent." It even makes you consider going to England just to hit on this guy's girls, but then you remember all the stereotypes and instead grab a tall cold Budweiser and celebrate your American heritage.

The Ol' Double Deuce

These guys are usually bartenders or bouncers who you barely recognize from earlier in the week, but there they are at another bar. They are there to have a good time, but they are scoping out the bar they are frequenting to see how it matches up to their establishment. They have to have a poker face walking around the bar so it doesn't look like they are having a good time. No one working there cares.

These guys rarely have a distinctive age that can be determined and love talking to other bouncers about fake ID's they busted that week. The ol' Double Deuce also feels that they deserve an extreme discount on drinks and promises the bartender they will hook them up at their place. Also to throw salt in the wound, due to the fact they work in the bar, they always have an in with all the promotional girls that come in to market the beer or liquor they work for.

When they are working they check out your ID's like you're an immigrant coming through Ellis Island. They will check holograms, the material the card is made of, scope out the picture like it's a Playboy centerfold to make sure it is you, and then they will ask for a backup and do the same with that. After they finally get through two ID's they will swipe your driver's license to verify exactly what the other 30 people waiting in line after you could tell, that you are 21 or over. These guys like to give off the impression that they are an elite group of identification specialists; a trait that can be learned by an idiot in a 10 minute tutorial video free at your DMV or alcohol board headquarters.

The Scarecrow

This guy will probably be a pretty cool guy, but is related to the Obscure Music Lover in this list in some way. The scarecrow is the guy who likes to buy women's jeans and wear a studded belt, just like the girl that you're checking out across the bar. You don't know why he wears lady jeans seeing that they pinch in inconvenient places, but this guy seems to think they are the cat's meow. Now don't get me wrong; this guy will probably be pretty laid back to the point where you could never have a physical confrontation with him.

The problem is his fashion of girls jeans, weird Easter colored pastel t-shirts with vintage subject matter on it, a beanie regardless of the temperature and glasses that he looks like he stole from his grandfather's old medicine cabinet. Also another looming problem is that anytime this guy sits his pastel colored shirt will always rise either showing off his mid-drift or lower back. As men, over the past 30 or so years our eyes have been trained to check out exposed mid-drift when it comes out of the corner of the eye. The reason behind this is that the target is 98% of the time female. But the scarecrow represents the 2% minority that make you throw up a little in your mouth.

Eventually the scarecrow will have to get a real job and clean up his image that may or may not also include a dirty beard and shaggy hair. He will finally have to give into the image that he so despises, by wearing a shirt and tie every day. But don't worry in his spare time the old wardrobe that survived the move to the new job will resurface at some sort of tiny pub or bar concert. You'll know this because your buddy will start a story out with, "So does it make me gay that I checked out a guy's mid-drift, but I thought it was a girl." The answer is yes, and you know exactly the guy he is talking about.

Sleeveless Steve

The guy who despite the weather will wear a sleeveless shirt because everyone should be aware they lift, a lot. These are typically the guys who go into the gym and don't do any work on their cardiovascular endurance because it threatens their size. They simply walk, no strut, around the weight room glaring at other guys and staring down girls who are just there to get their workout done and leave. These guys usually have a gallon of water, gloves, a stupid haircut of some kind, never smile, and only lift insane amounts of weight to the point where I'm afraid of their internal organs popping out and they call out with a loud grunt to draw attention.

They are not body builders because they still love drinking tons of beer during the weekend, and they probably own a motorcycle and must carry the helmet around with them in the gym so everyone knows it. They have seen one too many *Fast and the Furious* movies and other fine pieces of poorly written cinema that blew its whole budget on effects, and not quality acting. Naturally they think fast cars and looking jacked is the way to attract women. Yes, it is; but only if women are just as dumb as you are.

It's Never Too Late to Improve Yourself Guy

This is the 35-year-old that went back to school, mostly night classes to better himself. After working for 17 years he had an epiphany at one of his son's little league games, which you also have to hear about all the time. His projects are always over achieved and he makes you look lazy, but only because he has three kids that help him work on the project on a Sunday while you're recovering from a monster party. This guy will probably ask 45 questions per class just so he can understand the assignment enough that he doesn't make a mistake on his typewriter in his den.

He will probably have a mullet or some out of style haircut and tell you how college kids have lost touch. He is probably from the area and will tell you about what it was like in town in the 1980's. He is also convinced the Internet will flop and we will all go back to life before computers. He may even tell you about strip clubs he went to 15 years ago while you're on a class trip until you fall asleep on the bus on the way back to campus.

I remember one particular guy I worked with on a project who was 42 years old. I was moved by his situation because he and his son used to work on his projects together. But one day I was caught off guard when I left him alone in the forest on a field trip for no more than two minutes and when I returned he had captured a brook trout in a zip-lock bag that he kept after eating his peanut butter sandwich his wife made him.

The Strange Ranger

The Strange Ranger always travels by himself and will invariably show up at 4 AM in the laundry room and talks your ear off. You're just in there to throw a pair of pants in the washer that some girl threw up on and here is this guy telling you about some offbeat music group or the Asian girl he is trying to pick up over the Internet. You are afraid to upset him however because he is not usually mentally stable and is tremendous at sneaking up on you in his Sketchers.

You only stay on this guy's good side because he is probably the guy who may own a gun in the dorms or he may collect Japanese swords for some unknown reason. He probably also likes some offbeat bands and movies which he will bring up often. It is possible he could ask you to watch them with him alone. He will also try to invite himself into your outings because he will constantly want to know what is going on and if he can come. Since you were given a conscience by an unknown force, you have a hard time saying no much to the chagrin of your buddies.

Even if you need to find the Strange Ranger he can't be reached because he doesn't own a cell phone citing it as too expensive. When you go by his room, he probably won't be there because he is out for a 12-mile walk that has no discernible destination. He simply pops into local establishments to eat dinner by himself or join a table he was not invited to if he spots someone he knows. Your best hope at reaching him is staying exactly where you are because he will probably be walking by very shortly.

John the Baptist

This guy will constantly make you feel bad about yourself because he is always doing volunteer work and going to church three days a week. He always asks you to come with him and wants to give you his testimonial so that you can change your life and join his church. Now don't get me wrong, I dig God and attend mass when I get the chance but this kid takes it to a new level. Regardless of the fact you went to Catholic Church your whole life he will try to turn you Baptist or Methodist because he wants to save you from damnation.

He will look at you funny when you talk about what happened to you the previous night while you were smashed at some girl's place. His sheer presence will be awkward for you as well as your buddies who were also with you the previous night. But you can't get mad at him because he is a nice guy, just gets on your nerves all the time with his shirts that look like a Jack Daniel's ad that is actually a bible verse close up. This kid has a whole collection of these shirts, which he feels are better now because it expresses his faith so the whole world knows.

You really do not know what he does in his spare time other than read the bible, because he never wants to come out with the guys. He is afraid he will fail his faith if he has a beer or two with his guy friends and stays out after midnight. This disappoints you because you can see where he would be an absolute blast coming out because he is not even remotely shy and will go talk to anyone. You feel like he is a wingman wasted.

The Non-Drinker

The non-drinker is the guy who can quietly bring the mood of a group down because he just sits there drinking a coke or a cup of water when you are lucky enough to get him to the bar. He does not hit on girls because feels immoral about doing so because they have been drinking. People will often ask him if he is the designated driver, but he lives within walking distance of the bar as does everyone else. No one understands his deal because drinking is not against his religion.

The non-drinker will probably never bring a girl back to your place either. He is like the old man by the swimming pool when you're a kid who never said anything to anyone but just smiled as all the kids had fun in the pool. He was dressed for the occasion to go swimming, but never jumped in; much like the non-drinker. The non-drinker was never an alcoholic at any point, but still likes to have a good time but makes you feel like a drunk while doing so.

Obscure Music Guy

This guy will seem like a good guy at first, then after a few drinks he will start commenting on the music. After a while he will start getting mad about the music they play there, calling it too commercial. You do not find it odd because it is the music that is played in every dance club and bar at colleges all over the country. You do not know what this guy was expecting when he decided to come out.

Eventually the conversation will turn to what type of music you say. If you say a band that someone else at the band has heard of, then it is too commercialized for this jackass. So if you start making up band names like "The Mock 4's" or "Chickenthroat" this guy will start associating with you and calm down and will tell you about bands that you are pretty sure he is the only fan of. He tells you to look them up on MySpace despite the fact that you don't have it. But his crap bands are sure to rock your socks off, don't worry he can burn you a CD (yes, a CD) if you want it. You politely decline his invitation, and hope to never talk about music again. But you know that this will be a chronic issue when this kid is out.

El Brodeo

This guy is a friend of yours who you invite out for a good time and to help with the group of two or three to pick up girls. This guy shows up with his entourage, the only problem with his entourage is its full of guys that you don't know. I'm not talking one or two extra guys, which you can deal with; I'm talking four to six random dudes that you now have to go around the horn and meet. It has turned your 3-4 guy sneak attack on the ladies into a full infantry onslaught on girls. Now you are rolling 8 deep and no group of girls in the club can match your numbers.

Worse yet this guy will always bring an "Anchor" or two who have absolutely no skills with women and is not a very handsome guy to begin with. The anchors usually just sit in the booth looking depressed about being there and go on and on about their profession and endless sports stories. Don't get me wrong, I love sports; but I don't want my night of tomcatting to turn into an episode of *Around The Horn*.

El Brodeo, whom you invited out for a good time has just placed himself in the doghouse and will surely be skipped for a couple weeks on your contact list despite his presence in town. You may even run into him later that week at another bar as he is probably with two girls that night. You just want to strangle him and ask why he did not bring the two girls instead of his dorky friends, but you stay cool and calm. But needless to say he has fallen in the wingman depth chart.

King of the Eight Foot-Lift

This guy is in perfect health and is carrying nothing other than a backpack. You kindly say hello to one another as you walk into the lobby of your building. You kind of have to go to the bathroom after a long walk home from class in the rain, but do you want to wait for the elevator? You look over and see the stairs right next to the lift for the elevator, but you live on the 8th floor of the building. So you continue to wait as the elevator creeps down to the ground level.

Now that you have gone through the change of temperatures and the body has been able to adjust you have to pee ten-fold and start to get uncomfortable. When the door opens you politely let the girls get out before you step in and click the "8" button. The gentlemen you were waiting with gets in and you ask him what floor so you can also pound the "Door Close" button. He says "2" and you look at him in a way like you did not hear what he said. He looks at you, smirks a little, gives you the "what's up" headshake, and hits "2".

You had been waiting in the lobby for two minutes for the elevator to come up while this jackass has been standing there twelve steps from his floor. Now he is making you wait through a stop, a door opening, possibly someone else boarding the elevator, and the pause for the door to shut again. All of this is going on while your bladder feels like it is going to explode. You want to punch him in the face, but you politely say, "Have a good day," and then mumble a swear as he is out of hearing range. You then do the pee dance in the elevator all the way to your apartment.

The Beer Bandit

This guy is a thief and he can end a party very quickly after he strikes. I've been to a couple of parties where the Beer Bandit has shown his face and stole the beer tap to the keg leaving us with an untapped keg, ending a party pretty damn quick. No one ever sees this guy strike for the beer tap, but occasionally you'll catch him in the act of stealing beer from the fridge or the keg in a large container such as an old milk jug. He plans on throwing it on his fridge and saving it for a rainy day because he is cheap, and who will notice a gallon of missing beer?

You've never seen the Beer Bandit throw a party or offer anyone else one of his cheap beers he brings once someone confronts him for drinking other people's better quality long neck brews. This guy will buy a $6 12-pack of the cheapest beer he can find and put it in the fridge and his eyes fill with envy with other beers he sees at the BYOB event. He will first grab a Miller Lite, a common beer that anyone could have brought to the event, and probably won't be noticed. But with each passing round he gets greedier each trip he makes back to the fridge, because next it's a Budweiser, then a Molson, then a Guinness.

Throughout the time of this beer thievery no one has touched his crappy cheap canned beer, because it is only a decoy he will use to try to trade someone for better quality beer if he is caught. Under his ideal conditions he gets about six or seven high quality beers in his system before he starts drinking his mule urine tasting beer, because he probably won't taste it. Also everyone will see him and remember him carrying good beers, not the crap he actually bought when everyone is drunk.

The Senator

The Senator turns every conversation from fun to a debate over politics. There is absolutely no way to win this argument because you will surely be interrupted multiple times on your way to getting out of this conversation. The Senator always interrupts you and constantly points out your ignorance of vague pointless details that no one should be bringing up at a college party. Naturally, he feels that constant interruptions are the correct way to converse because he watches lots of C-Span, Fox News and MSNBC in his spare time.

You will never get out of a conversation with the Senator in anything less than a half hour because he has to go through his whole routine and stance for you. Even if he can sense that you want to leave and do not care about what he has to say he will continue to corner you until he is finished, much like a dog before it is fixed. It is better to just let him finish if you get stuck in his spider web of political jargon than to fight your way out. Try to keep everything to a nod and a "yeah" even if you disagree with what he has to say.

I once made the mistake of telling a Senator that I don't believe in voting for President. I was stuck at a desk for an hour being lectured of my rights and responsibilities as an American. I would have been there longer but I told the kid that I had to go take a call for a phone interview. Actually, I went up and watched *Seinfeld* during the afternoon instead. What is important to know is to find certain buttons that people have that make them go on and on about an unimportant subject for hours and avoid those buttons.

The Doc Brown

This guy lives in his past accomplishments despite being in college and even wears his high school letterman jacket around campus. He is a billboard for his region and his past, refusing to give up hope that he believes he is instantaneously a big man on campus. He tells you about how he was the team captain of his football team three years after he graduated and about games you couldn't care less about. If he does decide to stay the weekend and not return to his hometown, he will constantly compare his high school to other schools from people around the room. Regardless of your schools qualifications and accomplishments it doesn't match up to old East High School.

He probably still has the same girlfriend he had in high school if she is also a Doc Brown who also refuses to let go of the past and move on. Most likely these two will breakup at some point because they realize they need to get a life and their past accomplishments no longer are worth the paper they are written on. They will most likely get married and move back to the same school district they are from and never leave the region again. Getting out of their bubble is far too troubling for them to ever go through again.

The Constantly Paranoid Party Guy

This guy is generally a good guy but if there is any sense of danger in the air this guy sniffs it and assumes cops from the three surrounding counties are barricading on the apartment. If it is drinking in the dorms, this guy must have an air spray can and a heavy object against the door as a barricade. This guy believes police officers stop by dorms to make random stops to check on what college students are doing. If someone knocks on the door you better bet that this will be the first guy opening up the window or jumping into the closet.

The laughable thing about the whole Paranoid Guy is the first time someone finally convinces him to take a drink of alcohol there will be a bust next door and the cops will come knocking and hand him an underage as well. Once this happens, he will worry about what his parents will think and how they will be disappointed in him only to find out that his parents don't care. As long as he doesn't do something really dumb they expect him to drink at college, but he still can't grasp this concept.

Curve Crusher

This kid is usually the person in class who sits in the front row of the room in out of fashion clothes and asks a million questions to the annoyance of the teacher. They want to make darn sure they will get every participation point that they can, while you're in the back checking out the cleavage on a girl two seats to the right and couldn't care less. All you know is this guy is being the barrier between you getting out of class and getting back to your place for some leftover spaghetti and *The Price is Right.*

This kid has always been a pain in the side of other people for their entire existence. Now they are just a pain in the side for his roommate, who he always claims is too loud when he comes in at 11 PM on a Friday night to pick up the rest of his bottle of vodka. The saddest part is this kid has been in bed since 9:30 on a Friday night even as he hears people talking in the hall and yelling outside. But he doesn't even seem to be the least bit curious about the college social life.

When the professor decides to be a jerk and give a Monday morning test you are screwed because you were out all weekend. You threw together about two hour's worth of studying for a half semester's worth of information. Most of your notes are doodles and you seek out the Curve Crusher to take a look at his notes to scribble down some things here and there. But he refuses citing that you should have been paying attention and taken the notes when they were given.

He doesn't understand the concept of sharing and is caring because you would probably gladly take him out on the town to repay him. This isn't a big cost to you because he would probably be gone in about two drinks anyways. When the test does roll around Curve Crusher has been studying all weekend and scores a 98%, while the rest of a class who has a life gets an average of a 67%. Because of Curve Crusher's grade your test can only be boosted 2%. You decide not to push him in a trash can on the way out, relaxing in the fact that he will never make money because no one will want to hire him after interviewing this nerd.

Grad School or the Job Market?

This will be a tough question to answer and one you will surprisingly ask yourself upon graduation. Despite your grades that you got in your degree as an undergraduate, it really won't matter when it comes to a human resource worker's desk. All they really care about is you getting the degree, experience in related companies, and what type of person you are. The problem is it is too hard to put what type of person you are on one piece of paper like they demand your cover letters and resume should be.

You need to gauge how strong you are on paper for some dork sitting in an HR department to notice. This fatty better be having a good day because if they are out of maple glazed donuts on his way to work that just so happened to be the day your resume was received, well my friend you're screwed. This guy had to go with the sugar donut which will destroy you and 25 other people's chances of getting the job simply because he couldn't get that sweet maple nectar in his belly.

No longer is getting a job just knowing someone and then you start the next day. First, you had to graduate from high school to get a job, because only losers dropped out. But then they took it one step further and you needed a college or trade school degree to show you have any credibility; but eventually that wasn't even enough. Now we have to go through 5-7 years of school just to get the same place our ancestors got in much less time. It is frustrating to the extreme limits, so if you don't think that you will jump out on your cover letter and resume, then you probably should consider graduate school. But have a plan in mind; don't just go to extend your college days.

I knew that I was not overly impressive on my resume considering I had no actual writing experience outside of the classroom. I had spent two years in a radio booth, but once again no time outside of my school. I, instead, had worked for the Department of Transportation and at Beaver Stadium, which added nothing to my portfolio for my future in journalism. It was necessary for me to go to graduate school to be competitive in the job market.

When I started considering graduate school, I knew I wanted to eventually be a sports administrator at a large university because I enjoy the academic community and everything that comes with it. I started looking at graduate programs in the eastern United States with sports management and administration programs. Penn State, despite being one of the most athletic friendly colleges in the country, did not have such a program to allow me to stay. Forcing my hand, the search began to find a new school.

After about two months of searching programs I had it down to Old Dominion, Middle Tennessee State, Southern Mississippi, and Georgia Southern as my finalists. Since I've never been a fan of cold weather, going south made a lot of sense. After I took my GRE's the floodgates opened to send applications and be offered from schools. I was accepted into all of them, and some other schools came out of the woodwork like Tiffin University in Ohio and Maryland-Baltimore courting me. But I stuck to my guns and had it down to Old Dominion and Southern Miss because of their wonderful job of answering my questions. I settled on Southern Miss when I was offered a graduate assistantship.

When you take the GRE's the scores go to your current school and five other schools. Also, you're given the option to make the scores known to schools all over the country. You'd be a fool not to send the scores to five schools and not have them made known to every school in the country. Then you never know what you're going to get. Keep in mind that selecting a graduate school is not the same as undergraduate. In graduate school, the school picks you most times.

The key to getting a graduate assistantship to pay your tuition is research and staying on top of people. When a graduate assistantship passes their desk they will think of you because you have been on top of them throughout the whole process. I e-mailed department heads once a week asking if they had heard anything new, probably to their annoyance. But I got Southern Mississippi and Old Dominion interested enough to start putting together packages for me. I was happy with my decision, because I met tons of great people in graduate school.

But graduate school isn't for everyone. It's expensive if you don't get a scholarship or graduate assistant position of some kind and it's nothing like undergraduate life. Graduate school is more 75% a job and 25% like undergraduate life because you occasionally get to go party and play intramural Sports. You spend most of your hours set up by someone else like how a job is, and you get a little bit of flexibility on when you schedule your classes. But unlike undergraduate school you are expected to be there every class on time.

Some people are dying to get out of college and get in the work force. This is because they went to a small boring college or they want to have the comforts of a 30-year old at age 22. They often complain about not being able to find a job, but not wanting to sit in a classroom so they take some stupid job working at a Walgreen's and apply to jobs hoping a comet will hit the planet and knock off the other 100 more impressive applicants in front of them.

Internships suck in most cases because the first thing the guy that is making $60,000 a year does to figure out how to cut the budget is eliminate pay for interns. So have fun as you're constantly slapped in the face because you are competing with 200 other people over an unpaid internship, which is supposed to reward you with experience and college credit. If I really wanted to spend $3,000 to relocate and live in an apartment for six months while I don't get paid and work 40 hours a week I'd rather work at Burger King. Money is at a premium as a college student.

The problem is that when you're searching for an internship they want you to be enrolled in a university at the time. That's great, because you just graduated and now are looking for a job and don't even qualify. But you still don't have enough experience to get an entry level job; so you either luck into getting an internship because of a numbers game or you commit a crime and go to prison to get a job there in the wood shop.

You can always work in telemarketing or work in sales because these people are simply pawns doing all the work in the company. Most of the people do not make the cut and ever get a promotion and eventually burn out. Unless you have an iron will, stay away from these jobs that make you become who you hate. You're just about to sit down for dinner and watch Jeopardy when the phone rings and some jackass is on the line trying to ask you about your fabric softener and if you have enough time to listen to him about their product. If you recall from my description of the business major, this is the job that drives them to alcoholism.

Yet the people putting these postings together on a website not only have enough stones to say it is unpaid, but they demand an in-person interview and won't pay for your relocation or your transportation to the interview. From a kid who lives nowhere close to the white-collar jobs I've been groomed for, it is a Chuck Norris roundhouse kick to the face every time I read it. I don't even live close to a major airport without driving an hour and a half. I am often jealous of friends who live in large cities because of the many available jobs close to them.

If I come six hours driving or thirteen hours on the dirt bag infested Greyhound you better give me the job. When I get there I will struggle to find my way around and to the metro. I wouldn't know the first thing about riding on a subway because I've spent my life walking in my bare feet through the woods picking raspberries and blueberries. I'm just as uncomfortable in a city as a city person is out in the middle of no where.

Just send out as many applications as possible to jobs; the worst thing they can do is say no. But if you think graduate school will be beneficial to your career prospects by all means start the process and get the wheels moving. I would recommend trying to gauge where you are in your next to last semester in college. If the prospects don't look good for the job market or aren't what you expect, hit up graduate school. But go into school with a purpose of enhancing your resume.

You can't be afraid of people saying no. Once you leave college you'll probably hear it a lot from employers and colleges alike. Don't be discouraged and never stop improving yourself into a better professional. Just like any good thing, it takes time and little steps of improvement coming from good habits you do every day to pay off. Make sure you're disciplined and don't give up on your dreams.

Moving On After College

Depending on who you talk to you will get varying opinions about the subject of moving on to the real world following college. You have the people who were never really meant for the mold of college because they either weren't smart enough, sitting in a classroom wasn't for them, or the social aspects of college were just overwhelming. But for the other 85% of college students moving onto the real world, it is a difficult mountain to climb. No longer can you go to the bar every night and people brush it off by saying, "Don't worry he's just in college." Nope, as soon as you are no longer taking classes you become a drunk with a problem and people become very concerned.

Screw these people because they probably are just jealous because while they are playing scrabble with their 60-year-old neighbors you are out chasing down 21-year-old girls. Stay in the college atmosphere as long as possible, I'd say 26 or 27 is the limit before you start to become a creep. No one wants to go home from their job to sit there, be bored out of their mind and wait to sleep. You have plenty of time to do that when you are dead, so you need to keep the dream alive. Be social and get out to enjoy life.

You'll have the random friend who comes in and brags that they work hard and should be retired at 50. That's terrific for you because I'm going to have more fun between the ages of 22-25 then you ever will in your first four years of retirement at middle age. I do not even care if I am working a crappy job and barely getting by, my stories will be the ones people want to hear when we are 60. No stranger cares about your grand kids, they would much rather hear about you playing flip cup at age 24.

It is about having fun for as long as you can, because when you talk to friends who come back with their entry-level jobs they sound miserable because they can't cut loose anymore. You probably won't be making anywhere near the money they are, but they envy you most times because they find out life isn't about money. I had friends come back who have 50" TV's and nice apartments in the city who were jealous of me in my beer soaked and TV-less apartment. I got to extend my college social days by coming back for one last summer to State College and live glory days again after graduate school. To this day I'm not afraid to have a good time or feel I've grown out of it.

Don't get me wrong I would love to have a steady high paying job, but you have to do what you like to do otherwise every day will be a grind. It sounds nice to tell people you make $75,000 a year but if it is miserable for you, then why do it? These people see your life still living in a college town and going out to the bar three times a week for cheaper than what it costs them to go out once in New York or Washington D.C. But what they don't understand is that the college town is almost a living entity in itself.

The example that would be most appropriate of the three colleges I went to is State College. Despite your presence there are constant changes around you. As you know when you get older stuff gets taken from you. First it's friends, then athletic ability, metabolism, sometimes hair, and then you get old. But in the example of the town, it regenerates what it loses by replacing my friends that move away with incoming freshmen. But it is difficult to associate with freshmen obviously without looking like you're on To Catch a Predator.

While at Southern Mississippi, I had a number of friends who were freshmen, only because that was who I first met living on campus, and they were good friends with the guys I hung out with. But I started to realize that these kids were freshmen in high school when I started my first year at Penn State-Altoona way back in 2004. I sat there grizzled by long nights out on the town, long winter nights, working on my 9th semester of college; as I'm sitting there buttering my bread it puts me in a state of depression. I look at all the young faces around me and think, "Screw it, I'm going to continue rocking out,".

www.ingramcontent.com/pod-product-compliance
Lightning Source LLC
Chambersburg PA
CBHW060155070426
42447CB00033B/1456